Y0-EHC-936

The Flying Bridge Syndrome

ARLYNE O'GARA

As told to A. D. Pforr

Copyright © 2021 Arlyne O'Gara
All rights reserved
First Edition

PAGE PUBLISHING, INC.
Conneaut Lake, PA

First originally published by Page Publishing 2021

Cover: United States Merchant Marine Academy
logo and motto used by permission.
In order to assure personal privacy, many
fictitious names have been used.

ISBN 978-1-6624-4476-0 (pbk)
ISBN 978-1-6624-4477-7 (digital)

Printed in the United States of America

For the precious memory of William R. O'Gara
and Ida, Gordon, and Leneita.

.

When anxiety was great within me,
Your consolation brought joy to my soul

—Psalm 94:19

Contents

Preface

To my gracious readers:

You will be immersed in one special person's life experiences; the development of an incredible disease, Alzheimer's, and the way this one person dealt with the evolving and dreadfully persevering complications.

History books attest to the worth of past journey's importance in building a relational bridge through others' lives, issues, and voyages. Each of our missions on earth is personal, exclusive, and unique. Alzheimer's disease is, undeniably, relative to faith and love. You may even retrieve some hidden compensatory and profound jewels, shadowing forth a beneficent, generous, and bountiful journey. Basic to the journey is the flying bridge, the topmost part of a ship, which is taught to be emblematic toward always seeking one's best and striving for the top.

With the treasure of strengthening our spirit and touching our hearts, we totally accept the shortcomings of the person with Alzheimer's, who eventually and gratefully support us, with their warmth of holding hands, tender touch, smiling faces, and silent presence.

I introduce you to Captain William R. O'Gara.

Arlyne's Acknowledgments

What a wonderful opportunity to open my treasure chest of the wondrous people who brought sunshine into my life. The sunshine arrived in my life from many and varied sources.

The awesome support I received in its multiple forms came from the initial encouragement and steadfast belief in me. This came from Annette Kelly, PhD, MSN, ARNP, and Peggy Bargmann, BSN. For many years of togetherness with our combined interests in Alzheimer's disease always driving us, they were both my mentors. Annette, who was the past CEO of Central and North Florida Alzheimer's Association and outstanding community leader, and Pedgy, who was the founder of the successful Brain Fitness Academy, have lovingly given me the necessary strength to swim upstream.

For assurance and guidance, Gregory and Carolyn Hess were my stalwarts of unending sources. My eternal gratitude to Dr. Ira J. Goodman, neurologist and exceptional human being, who was a special blessing to me.

The understanding, suggestions, goodness, and comfort in shared memories were all so magnificently meaningful from such angels as David Odahowski and Mary Ellen Hutcheson (Edyth Bush Charitable Foundation), Captain James Tobin (US Merchant Marine Academy), Nora Cameron, Barbara Garside, Karin Noble, and Paul Waters. Their superb concerns, friendship, and love surely contributed to that swim upstream becoming a reality. I couldn't be more grateful, thankful, and blessed to have each of them in my life.

Each soul leaves a legacy of love,
Each memory a bridge to comfort and
Connect one heart to another forever.

William O'Gara, 1971

Lieutenant Commander William O'Gara, 1962

1

Life, Liberty, and the Pursuit of Happiness

His fifteen-year-old long and shapeless legs easily and quickly propelled him across the tiny sitting room to the lone window. He lifted the window frame with one preconceived resolution. To an uncaring sea of tenement buildings, he screamed to his immediate world, "I don't care what the neighbors think!"

Seldom a recalcitrant child, Billy had finally hit the saturation point, but never in his fifteen years had he ever raised his voice or shown any disrespect to his four-foot-high, diminutive, and now shocked mother.

"Billy, that's a terrible thing to do! You close that window!" Frozen to the spot, she said no more.

Anita, his mother, was his only parent and was a highly dependent person. She had no other children. A simple, loving parent, she was doing her utmost to best guide her responsible and loving son to maturity. With little to no education and very little income, this was an arduous daily task. Her husband, William, had long ago abandoned his masonry occupation and little family shortly within the first year of marriage in favor of the comfort that alcohol brought.

Having had the inherent German work ethic, Anita's parents were among the many families of that era who were the stalwarts of our fledgling, energetic country. Anita was the baby of six siblings and was constantly catered to and given any available attention. Consequently, she quickly realized the many advantages this indulgence gave her but was unaware that this precursor also limited schooling.

She met and married William, a six-foot Irishman and a mason (brick layer), which meant he could nicely provide the means of a satisfactory living. Urban life in this era mostly provided the accessibility and sociability of the many local bars. Soon, William became a nonentity to his little family, making only two short appearances in his son's life thereafter.

Government assistance programs scarcely met the little family's basic needs of living. After all, this was the difficult economical era of the 1920s. Anita was a dear, sweet, and healthy, little person but regarded herself as unqualified for employment because of the many imagined illnesses with which she struggled. At seven years of age, this provided Billy with his first efforts in entrepreneurship by making his own shoeshine box. At twelve, he got an after-school job at a printshop as a printer's devil or an apprentice, and the money he earned was, of course, immediately handed to his mother.

Meanwhile, Billy's mother was busy packing and unpacking on a regular basis, resulting in a minimum of sixteen apartments in twelve years. A positive aspect of city living did allow Billy lessons in making friends and participating in street games that children created. Close living quarters also made him ever aware of the nearness and consideration of others. Consequently, his mother's favored method of behavior control used on Billy was an overly worn mantra of "What will the neighbors say? What will the neighbors think?" The menu consisting of everything fried and tomato soup continued as the daily diet.

Fortuitously, Billy's buddies became his immediate world and would foretell a lifelong impact. Although a very ecumenical group of four, they each represented a separate heritage: Herman, the German; Mel, the Jew; Paulie, the Italian; and William, the Irishman.

Since Billy lived close to Mel, he became Mel's closest ally, spending many family hours of activities and meals together. Helping Mel prepare for his Bar Mitzvah also provided a special familial cement.

Herman and his family graciously invited Billy many times to join them in the summer when they visited the Jersey Shore. This was an extremely joyful journey for Billy.

This group produced a chemical engineer, a CPA, a corporation representative, and a business entrepreneur. The buddies would eventually find each other again and decide to have reunions, including wives, once a year and call themselves "The Kindergarteners."

They were a wondrous, outstanding, and blessed collection of people who grew a closeness few people would ever enjoy. They were an incredible collection of very special people who greatly enjoyed each other. One could argue that the boyhood summers of nonstop pinochle playing might have been the basis and the glue that indelibly underlined the best of childhood memories for each.

At fifteen years of age, and almost six feet tall, Billy was ready to assert some normal innermost teenage feelings. He loved his mother and felt the need for her protection, but he also was feeling suffocated by her dominance and dependency. How would he ever be able to weigh, or forget, her favorite and familiar utterances: "You will always take care of me, won't you, Billy? Perhaps you could become a truck driver and then you would be able to come home often."

The Kindergarteners
Right to left: Mel Bleemer, Hermann Reinhold,
Paul Puleo, and William O'Gara, 1985

William and Peppy, 1983

Billy and Bill, 1994

2

Hardship Is a Great Teacher

With the ever-pressing need for money, Billy left school in his junior year, lied about his age, and was accepted into the Merchant Marines. It was 1945, and he was seventeen years of age. However, at the conclusion of one year with the Merchant Marines, he arrived at a fateful decision. The reality of the onerous seagoing requirements and, at times, life-threatening effort during World War II did not fulfill his expected view of romantic adventures. A worthwhile lesson well-learned.

Bill returned to school and acquired his high school diploma. During his frequent bus riding to and from school, he was scanning all the advertisements positioned in the ceiling of the bus when one advertisement, specifically and especially, caught his attention with the word "free." Merchant Marines was offering a four-year education, not only free but added "a small, monthly stipend." What transpired after this chance event became the first day of the rest of his life. He would be able to get an education and still provide, monetarily, for his mother, which he did. Keeping two dollars a month for himself, he sent the balance home to Anita.

After the initial required and successful testing, plus a US senator's recommendation, Bill headed for the United States Merchant Marine Academy (USMMA) at Long Island, New York, one of the five United States federal academies.

Steamboat road, here I come!

The strict regulations of military life quickly gathered around him amid the stringent physical and educational rules. Having an innate affable but gregarious personality, he soon adjusted to the midshipmen's strictly held behavior. This included responsibility, respect, expectations, scheduling, preparedness, and a variety of other regimental regulations. The emphasis on an educationally high performance was held in enviable esteem but not without "Heads up, shoulders back, chin in" as he entered his future.

Anchors aweigh!

Beginning cadet time was generally a difficult and, perhaps, a shockingly adaptive period for most, and it was not without the loathsome expectations of punctuality. Competently sustaining the spectrum of challenges, including spending a year at sea and, incidentally, becoming a successful cross-country runner, Bill became a 1950 graduate marine engineer of the US Merchant Marine Academy. He was then accepted into the US Navy as an ensign. Another stroke of God's touch, he thankfully prayed.

Aye, aye, Ensign, full speed ahead!

The Navy presented numerous challenges in which Bill thrived. His tested high IQ would surely advance him in this realm, which he wholly enjoyed. Assignments to Korea and many months in Italy could have been exceptions, however.

His sense of humor, concern for others, candor, but lover of truth, traveling, and a never-ending curiosity were all reflected in his demeanor and future attainments. He was, indeed, a happy captain in the US Navy.

Aye, aye, sir!

3

Finding a Reason for Being

Making use of his Navy experience and coinciding with his current employment, he attended and earned a master of business administration (MBA) from Wharton School of Business at the University of Pennsylvania in Philadelphia. Employed at the same time, he was also a finance administrator in a nearby correctional farm school. While a hospital administrator at Saint Francis Hospital in New York, he obtained a master's degree in public administration from New York University. All this educational preparation gave background impetus in seeking worthwhile future employment and endeavors.

Successful and meaningful experiences of several years in hospital administration at Philadelphia Misericordia and Sacred Heart Hospitals actually spawned the inspirational birth and background of Bill's first attempt at forming a company.

Prison Health Services (PHS), the first of its kind in the United States, provided basic health services to prisoners, setting up services to eliminate changes at the local level. It set up complete care in every medical aspect of the prisoner. Following was Ships Parts Inc. (SPI), which produced spare parts and repair parts for US Navy vessels. Both companies enjoyed outstanding successes. The added adjunct of Personnel Management Services (PMS) quickly followed, giving valued strength and support to the previous two businesses.

Demonstrating obvious outstanding qualities as a committed, successful, and forward-bound administrator, Bill was held in high esteem by each of his partners in all the businesses (PHS, SPI, and PMS). Each was a fifty-fifty partnership, reflecting his innate honesty, easy adjustment to circumstances with savoir faire, patience, determination, and understanding—sometimes despite the cost. Horatio Alger incarnate!

Bill's earlier and continued quest for ongoing education found him attending a Russian language class in a nearby university. Spanish was already an achievement for him, and he spoke it well. He enrolled for the Russian class as a challenge and actually as an alternative. He really arrived there to enroll as a French student. Fate intervened because those classes were filled, and the alternative, open language class was Russian. Consequently, Russian class it was.

It didn't take very long before the gregarious Bill was engaging the various students in conversation and pleasantries of acquaintanceship. There was no pressure of having to pass this course, but of course, he would. Life was to be enjoyed.

The evening that Russian class assembled, Bill couldn't help being attracted to this quiet female student who was nicely attired in a simplistic fashion, was attractive, and was about five feet, five inches. She projected self-reliance and purpose of presence, which helped to preclude any present opportunity to become acquainted.

After a few classes had elapsed and a blasting fire alarm shattered classroom decorum, the opportunity was at hand for Bill to approach this lovely lady. He positioned himself in line formation next to this fair lady, whom he wanted to meet. In a few moments, he had softly and gentlemanly introduced himself. "Hi, my name is William, and I've wanted to make your acquaintance. I hope you will forgive my forwardness."

Volunteering only minimal information to him, she said that she was Arlyne, a secondary school teacher of German and English languages, and was now attempting to broaden her language skills.

Enter Arlyne

Future classes allowed their acquaintance to blossom from the initial invitation of "Could we have coffee at a nearby diner after class?" Although momentarily and initially uncomfortable, Arlyne hesitated but then agreed.

Her first impression of the six-foot-tall attractive man, however, was not immediately all positive to Arlyne. She wasn't quite sure as she observed his jovial and friendly behavior toward most everyone. As the friendship grew, she discerned William (not Bill or Billy) to have many admirable qualities. He was kind, thoughtful, considerate, trustworthy, always gentlemanly, and polite. Discovered at a later date, he was also ambitious, contemplative but gregarious, and purposeful; he also had a profound, valued, and private reverence, and these were all positive and admirable qualities. In fact, she thought he was almost perfect.

Over time, the relationship progressed from low gear to expectations of a joyful future together.

Time together multiplied, strengthened, and generated wondrous social participation, like going to the theater, seeing the ballet, going to the opera, running, swimming, and dining at endless restaurants. These were such happy, valued times together that surely no one else could possibly have experienced, she mused delightedly. How could anyone be so magnificently blessed?

Arlyne realized, with unconditional assurance, that their love and togetherness were, indeed, complete and that marriage was the next, inevitable step. And so the enviable marriage journey blossomed into a flourishing and prosperous future. Arlyne prayed reverently and thankfully that they truly had been blessed by bringing them together with a special love and relationship. They must be mindful and grateful forever by holding these gifts sacred and holding each other's hands eternally.

Amen

As the calendar's months and years raced swiftly by, Arlyne thoughtfully reviewed the exciting multitude of happy, outstandingly positive, and unique events, and also the sparseness of unhappy, mediocre, and perhaps seldom wretched circumstances. Life's ups and downs of raising two cherished and loved children to adulthood; experiencing the passing of Anita, William's mother; and losing Arlyne's mother and father were all part and parcel of life's experiences.

Arlyne's diligent accomplishments of a BA degree at West Chester University, a Villanova University master's degree, and a doctorate (PhD) earned through Temple University and Brunel University (Uxbridge), England, resulted in her becoming a secondary school principal. Combined with William's educational background, this would contribute to the direction of their future exploration, having a total of six graduate degrees between them.

Ships Parts Inc. (SPI) was situated in California. This was home to William's partner and was, therefore, chosen to be home base for the business (1982). The partner had been William's roomie many years earlier at USMMA. He had experience in the Navy's needs for used and spare parts for ships. SPI was a wonderfully successful business for eight years. The end of the Persian Gulf War, unfortunately, determined the end of SPI. The government's decision was to mothball many US ships, and therefore, it concluded contracts as well. It was a marvelous and worthwhile experience.

Prison Health Services (PHS) was, indeed, a completely, albeit wonderful, historical and quite different journey (1979).

Operationally, with Personnel Management Services (PMS), Arlyne's company responsibilities included both businesses by having capable employees who completed payrolls, made state and federal timely reports, made appointments, and tended to the other numerous details, making a definitely busy office. William and Arlyne worked together, as always, writing and assembling the personnel policies and procedures manuals for each of the companies. Of course, lawyers were included to keep everything safely legal.

PHS grew at a rapid pace, to include many other state prisons, which eventually meant air travel would be a requirement. However, local prison contracts remained to be serviced as well.

An appointment for Arlyne with the warden of a local county prison became an event not to be forgotten. Upon entering the prison, Arlyne heard the heavy clanking of the locked doors behind her and was told by the pleasant corrections officer at the desk that another officer would escort her to the mess hall and kitchen. The escort officer, a six-foot-three and 185-pound young man, entered and stopped in his tracks.

"Frau, what are you doing here?" This was a student from Arlyne's former high school class.

He escorted her through the mess hall to the kitchen, where well-behaved inmates, in whites, were working. A voice from across the kitchen hollered, "Frau, what are you doing here?"

It was from another student from her high school class but an inmate. He explained his presence after she asked what he was doing there. Before leaving the facility, Arlyne had met two corrections officers and two inmates from her teaching days. A special and unusual place for a reunion, wouldn't you say?

Arlyne quickly learned how to pack suitcases to meet challenges with even the shortest notification. One morning while having coffee, William softly addressed Arlyne by saying, "What is your schedule today?"

She knew she was going to be asked for a favor. After relating that she had an appointment with a local county warden, he again said sweetly, "I think it would be best if you got a plane ticket this morning and fly to Daytona, Florida, to attend a bidding conference there."

Guess where she was that afternoon? A carbon copy of many other days.

All hands on deck!

The days ahead were generally heavily scheduled. Because both William and Arlyne were equal working and collaborative officers for all the businesses, they soon realized their love, respect, and dependency for each other only grew as the business grew to greater heights.

William, of course, was the driving force with a presence of mind that easily grasped business situations. He had an almost genius proclivity to quickly assess advantages, disadvantages, assets, debits, taxes, liabilities, as well as many other aspects of operating a successful business. After all, he was erudite and felt strongly that these were the necessary games you needed to play to reach the flying bridge in all cases. The flying bridge is the highest point of any sailing vessel, and he was a Navy man.

He was well-equipped with self-control, unruffled tolerance, and efficiency to deal with the presented challenges of the business world. Always the articulate gentleman, always aware of his personal presentation, always "head up, shoulder back, chin in," never arrogant, and never denigrating anyone—these showcased his personal and business acumen and acceptance. One breathtaking exception occurred, however, to his never saying anything negative about any person. He once referred to a close business associate's demanding, dissatisfied, vociferous, and ever-complaining wife as the "Bitch von Buchenwald." That truly was an exploding bombshell exception. After all, no one is perfect.

Qualifications also became imperatively supported with increasing travel to and from required meetings, exemplifying the need for efficacy. Travel became multiplied and vital, as the companies' contracts grew to fifteen states, which were serviced by PHS and with additional responsibilities to the Navy. Personal enjoyment of travel was an added factor.

The quiescence of a rather routine life of the past, and only occasionally, a nomadic life, began to fade. Business-life requirements continued on, but now, some newly proposed responsibilities from abroad came into focus. Actually, this development presented the impetus and opportunity to also satisfy this couple's burning curiosity and profound historical interests in other countries.

Bon voyage!

The year 1972 began the planning of an entirely new and alternate beginning into a traveling realm. They found it not only exciting, explorative, and deeply mystifying but also tremendously informative and gratifying. A wonderful new challenge.

They realized and agreed that there were basically so many places they both wanted to investigate for so many reasons. Educationally, they agreed to the need for documentation for later referential review and enjoyment as well. Consequently, the following is a log, a descriptive travelogue, of most places they visited. There were few additional explorations not documented, however.

The excitement of future adventures together would be carefully preplanned and thoroughly documented with descriptions and information they both deemed necessary and appropriate for future review.

William enjoyed the challenge of planning all the travels and did an excellent job. Up to this point in their lives together, William profoundly desired that all the joys and challenges must be a shared adventure. So it was, and so it shall be, forever holding each other's hands.

Travelogue

Germany, 1973

Visiting East and West Germany brought back many memories of previous experiences in West Germany during the occupation era and after World War II (1966). After World War II and during the US military occupation at Bremerhaven, Northern Germany, a Brotherhood Week was declared. The person was to bring American and West German relationships together and to share a variety of planned activities. One such activity was an evening gala of dancing, with emphasis on the waltz. Prince Louis Frederick, son of the kaiser, and Olivia de Haviland were special guests. A thrill and shock of a lifetime for Arlyne was when Prince Louis asked her to dance a waltz with him. An honor and a tremendously special experience that was never to be duplicated or forgotten.

Harkening back to these occupation days, Germany was divided into East Germany, which was controlled by Russia, and West Germany, which was controlled by the United States and England.

The city of Berlin was divided into four regions controlled by the individual countries of France, England, USA, and Russia. Traveling to West Berlin from West Germany was a restrictive effort. One had few choices where to travel and how to travel—through or across Russian-controlled East Germany. Three air traffic lanes and one railroad were the extent of allowed availability to travel any of these avenues, and then you must have travel orders. By land, there was one route across East Germany, and you must be sure to remain on it.

A visit to East Berlin from West Berlin meant access through the Brandenburg Gate (Russian controlled) by bus and meant no cameras. It was an instant replay of the war's destruction. Skeletal bombed-out buildings and sidewalks piled high with debris made any sidewalk impassable. It truly seemed as if the bombing occurred yesterday. Arlyne never divulged how she had some 35 mm slides of Hitler's cement bunker that had been retrieved from underground and was presently setting atop the ground.

By 1973, and by contrast, West Germany had a lot of new construction of modern thoroughfares and buildings, and obviously, had many business activities. A new and thriving country. The decision, as part of this revisit, was to include Berlin on the agenda. Of course, if going by car to reach West Berlin, it was still necessary to enter the Russian-controlled East Germany territory and to remain only on the route indicated. It was heavily surveilled the entire distance to Berlin. Arriving in West Berlin, it was required to drive over mirrors and to endure a thorough investigation of all identifications.

Berlin was a new city rebuilt beautifully for the most part, with portions still evident of the past heavy repercussions. One such example was the *Gedachtnis Kirche* (memorial church) in mid-city. This had been a beautiful large church but was heavily bombed. During occupation, a portion of the church was saved and repaired with much care. Consequently, the memorial church stands as a definite reminder of a violent past.

By contrast, West Berlin was a shining new city with a bustling populace of productivity while East Berlin's Russian-controlled area shouted of a land forgotten.

The next decision was to drive north and follow the border that divides East Germany (Russia) from West Germany (Deutsches Democratishe Republic). So many stories had evolved regarding this threatening border attempting to keep Germans from escaping to West Germany. William and Arlyne's curiosity needed to be satisfied, and they decided to follow this border, traveling south with their rented car but on the West German side, of course. All along there were guard dogs, trucks with soldiers, cannons pointed eastward, floodlights, dragon teeth, and several areas of no-man's-land. These were only some of the varied efforts to keep Germans from escaping to the West. A tremendously impressive and distressful scenario.

Still following the border, it was time for a stop to stretch their legs. William and Arlyne got out of the car and stood gazing at this border only about twenty-five feet straight to the East. Arlyne was pondering the fact that this border represented such forced confinement for so many people, when a sudden roar of a truck engine filled the air. A truck with three armed Russian soldiers in the rear appeared on the East German land, stopped in front of them, and seemed to have come from nowhere. Everything became very quiet and still. William and Arlyne were more than stunned. Both of them froze to the spot. Arlyne finally pleaded with William, "Now what do we do?"

And without hesitation, he replied, "Everybody wave!"

And wave they did. It was obviously a surprise to the guards. Nonplussed, the guards in the truck remained for a few moments and then very slowly drove away. A very welcomed deep breath of relief filled the air.

While in the area of Southern Germany, they wanted to revisit many of the Bavarian historic sites. At the foot of the Alps were such beautiful and scenic areas: Oberammergau, where every ten years, the Passion Play is enacted; Garmisch Partenkirchen, where the 1936 Olympics was held; Munich, now the capital; Berechtsgarten; and the Hitler Eagles Nest near Austria.

Farther to the East were Vienna, home of the renowned Saint Stephen's Boys Choir; Opera House, which was newly built, having been leveled during World War II; Salzburg, with the underground caves of salt mines; and the romantic Danube River. This area was also home to many palaces (schlosses) built by the passions of crazy King Ludwig II, Herrenchiemsee, Linderhof, and Neuschwanstein, to name but a few. A magnificent absorption and remembrance of previous travels, and they were loving every moment.

A sad auf Wiedersehen.

Ireland, 1974

In 1974, Ireland became the chosen point of interest. Shannon, Ring of Kerry, and Waterford began the odyssey. A fortunate experience began at the Dublin Horse Show, where they met some Irish natives who insisted that William and Arlyne should visit Northern Ireland, where most of the current fighting and bombings were occurring between the British and the IRA. A wonderful but daring challenge.

Before beginning this journey, Arlyne wanted to make a phone call to her dear friend Sister Belinda in Kilkenny, located quite near Dublin. Sister Belinda and Arlyne's friendship was born when they were both master's degree candidates at Villanova University in 1965. Both continued to be the only females in most classes, which cemented their friendship. Upon receiving their degrees, Sister Belinda, who had been residing at the local convent, returned to Kilkenny, Ireland, to become principal of her 6–12 Manor House School (the Royal and Prior Comprehensive School).

Sister Belinda was euphoric to receive Arlyne's phone call and invited William and Arlyne to join her convent sisters for lunch, plus a visit to her school. At lunch in the convent, they sat on benches at the table. Over a lovely lunch, plus wine, William was his gregarious self and thoroughly enjoyed the entire experience, as did the nuns.

The sister sitting next to Arlyne nudged Arlyne with an elbow, remarking, "We don't have wine every day." It was all a tremendous gift.

They were not yet finished with Ireland, and on they went to Belfast, in Northern Ireland. Approaching Belfast, they were prevented from entering the city, an exclusion to everyone. A parking lot was provided at the outskirts with military escort or bicycle.

Once in the city, only open jeeps with English soldiers patrolled the streets. Shopping was a unique experience. Everyone, including babies and baby carriages, was bodychecked for bombs before entering any store.

"Guess they aren't concerned about store theft," William tartly remarked after observing no bodycheck was made upon exiting the store.

They were driving toward Londonderry, still in Northern Ireland, and enjoying the rather lovely countryside and the narrow country roads when suddenly, two men with guns rushed into the center of the road just ahead of their car. They were instructed to open the trunk of their car for a search. Satisfied that they were not carrying any ammunition or guns, the guards allowed them to continue on their way.

It was not an interruption without a great deal of apprehension, to say the least, but they continued toward their destination of Londonderry.

Londonderry was another northern city in Ireland that was completely devoid of any human beings in the streets. To gain admittance required a car check of driving over mirrors and ignoring giant signs that shouted, "No extradition! British troops out!"

Leaving the North, William wanted to find his ancestral beginnings in County Sligo. Gratefully, it was a celebratory and joyful day that he found some O'Garas there. A fun, rewarding, and successful effort. Their curiosity was in full bloom to discover and explore more dolmans. The dolmans were usually huge prehistoric rocks of various arrangements, the meaning of which remains nebulous. They seemed to be everywhere, and strangely, no one paid much attention to any of them. In a very pastoral setting, William and Arlyne spied a lone large dolman in a distant pasture. They climbed fences, scaled stonewalls, and stared down some startled cattle to arrive at the lone huge dolman. They must have had some sort of meaning but for whom or for what? What, no hot dog stand!

The beautiful green land and serene countryside of high crosses; dolmans; sheep what was wandering all over and stopping mostly in the middle of the road; and horse-drawn carts in proliferation made unforgettable memories.

Slan! (Goodbye!)

England, 1976–1977

Windsor Castle was a fifteen-minute ride from Brunel University, Uxbridge, which was located in West London. Brunel was a temporary residence for Arlyne when she was completing courses for her doctorate degree. She was initially properly impressed, having learned one of her dormitory residents Jim was a brother to actor

Joseph Cotton, one of her all-time favorites. Jim was working on his psychology doctorate, and it wasn't long before she made determined efforts to avoid his presence.

A favorite haunt became Westminster Abbey, in the heart of London, and this presented the opportunity for William and Arlyne to complete a sarcophagus rubbing of a thirteenth-century knight, the second oldest sarcophagus in the British Empire. Of course, Buckingham Palace and Christopher Wren's Saint Paul's Cathedral were the stalwarts. Some side trips were also extra special, such as Stonehenge, Cheddar, Shakespeare's home areas, Southampton (*Queen Elizabeth II* docking), and Glasgow, Scotland, to name only a few.

Cheerio! Ta-ta!

During this time, Arlyne realized being away from home became very difficult. Missing William became almost more than she could handle. She flew back home to write her dissertation, and once again, she was faced with a busy business schedule as well.

Korea, Hong Kong, and Japan

Now, it was again the urge to travel that dictated the days ahead, coinciding with an appointment to touch base with William's friend in Seoul, Korea. However, this journey included Japan and Hong Kong, too—all highly interesting but seemed all greatly overcrowded for a country girl. Who could ever forget the Japanese Ginza, Nara Park, the bullet train, and the Kabuki (theater)!

Sayonara!

Guatemala, 1977

William and Arlyne flew to Guatemala on December 1978, and it was interesting and challenging, to say the least. Upon landing, soldiers with guns greeted their arrival at the end of the runway.

William grumbled under his breath, "We really didn't expect a brass band!"

Guatemala City was the capital, with military guards on most street corners.

This adventure began immediately upon renting a car. Approximately two blocks out of Guatemala City, they encountered dirt roads forever and a junglelike environment. Occasionally, they would pass a few mud-thatched homes, complete with stopping for children, chickens, and pigs to scatter from the center of the roadway. Laundry needs were based in the nearby creeks. Fuel for cooking there were tied bunches of sticks or twigs carried and balanced atop the natives' heads. There were no bridges; consequently, if one met a deep creek and had a low-type car, one would indeed be in trouble.

The appointed destination was British Honduras, later called Honduras; and at long last, they were nearing the border. First, however, they decided to stop and stay overnight at the largest town with the most inhabitants they had yet seen. A huge and beautiful stone church was the centerpiece of the town, with busy kiosks selling goods surrounding the church walls; this comprised the entire town.

They searched for a motel, but that was just not available. Finally, they did find a room for rent, six feet by eight feet, furnished with a single-size bed and one small end table holding one tiny lamp. Sleep was not forthcoming when they both bolted to an upright position when the church bells exploded like an atomic bomb to announce it was 6:00 a.m.

Visiting the inside of the beautiful, tremendously large church before they left was a must. Entering, they mainly saw a vast area of an attractively tiled floor and not a pew or a chair in sight. If you desired a candle, one had to light the candle and drip some melted candle on the floor to hold the candle. Meanwhile, the local dogs wandered in and out to make your acquaintance.

Continuing their journey to the British Honduras border was imminent. Presenting all their passports, documents of identification, and orders to the guards was a gratified feeling at last to have arrived. A sigh of relief was definitely appropriate.

The guards, with stern, frozen faces, just stared at them carefully and slowly, nicely folded all their papers, handed them to William, and firmly stated, "You must turn around here, and you will not be allowed into our country."

Chalk this one up to zero. So what to do next, for there was no opportunity but to retreat?

The only decision available with the present circumstances was to try to find their way to Chichicastenango and hope for an airport. On the way, there were many mud volcanoes; however, that were dormant, but there were many churches and other buildings vacated due to earthquakes.

At last, they found a small airport with small planes. They were told the plane would take off in an hour. Three hours later, they were finally airborne.

Adios, amigos!

Russia, 1979

The master plan for future trips continued, sandwiched between the many responsibilities of their business operations. In 1979, a journey to Russia was scheduled, and it was the United Socialist Soviet Republic (USSR). The flight, via Aeroflot Airways, seemed interminable before landing in Leningrad (USSR). This city was later (1991) returned to its original name, Saint Petersburg. The Neva River flowing through Leningrad was usually frozen over from November to March and would have snow until May with the usual ten to twenty degrees. This area was so close to the Arctic Circle that it had only a brief period of twilight intervening between sunset and sunrise.

The Russian Hermitage Mansion was the Winter Palace in Leningrad, 1764, by Catherine the Great and home of the Russian czars. Now it is known as the largest museum in the world, with a wealth of outstanding architecture, inside and outside.

The bus trip to Moscow, Russia, was a lengthy but necessary trip to reach the country's historical showplace. Traveling south, however, was interrupted to acknowledge the famous Volga River, which was frozen over. William and Arlyne enjoyed the fact that they had never known anyone to have walked on the Volga River, but they did.

They arrived in Moscow amid a group of children huddled together at the bus door asking for chewing gum. There were also questions for blue jeans at almost any price. Having at last arrived in Moscow, it was almost unreal to observe the actual existence of the Red Square and its immensity. This tremendous expanse included the beautiful Saint Basil's Cathedral radiating its outstanding onion dome architecture. The lines of people waiting to view Lenin lying in state extended as far as one could see and then some. Yes, they did. Actually, there were lines of people at all individual stores that sold anything—bread, milk, or coffee. There were electric trains and streetcars. Subways were shockingly and outstandingly impressive, with bright lighting, gleaming cleanliness, and a marvelous array of hanging art throughout these underground walkways.

After registering at the Intourist Hotel, they found the accommodations very basic. The room was stark and devoid of any pretense of sumptuous furnishings. Alas, they were thankful for the basics. To know you were being wiretapped didn't require an Einstein.

The more familiar names associated with Russia would be composers Pyotr Tchaikovsky and Dmitry Shostakovich; ballet dancers Rudolf Nureyev and Mikhail Baryshnikov; and authors Aleksandr Pushkin and Fyodor Dostoyevsky, to name a few.

One must remember to bargain when shopping, and most churches went underground and outwardly became libraries at this time.

William and Arlyne were rather eager to say *paka paka* or *dasvidaniya*!

Le Havre, France, 1980

William wanted a visit to Le Havre to walk down memory lane. He had spent some days here during World War II. A city of Normandy, it is renowned for its placement of port shoreline and maritime history. It is an outlet of France's Seine River and quite international.

Scandinavia, 1981

Copenhagen is the capital city of Denmark, bordered by the North Sea and the Baltic Sea. Its port location has determined its international or urban flavor because it seems to be mid-stopover to other northern countries. Hans Christian Andersen is notable for his stories. A statue of a mermaid sits on a rock in the bay, supposedly waiting for her prince to come from Sweden to rescue her.

Stockholm is the capital of Sweden, a Scandinavian archipelago of fourteen islands. Their royal palace has more than six hundred rooms since 1523, a changing of the guards, cobblestone streets, waterfront pathways, and preserved ships in the VASA museum, which were all delightful. Warm clothes are a must.

Oslo is now the capital of Norway. But at one time, it was a part of Sweden, and still earlier, it was a part of Denmark. But foremost and always, it is a maritime nation. Some notables are Leif Erikson, a notable Viking; Henrik Ibsen, a playwright; Edvard Grieg, a composer. There were the Viking Ship Museum, which had vessels from the ninth and tenth century; Kon-Tiki Museum, with an actual raft of Thor Heyerdahl used to sail the Pacific from South America to Polynesia; and the Nobel Peace Prize's home. Norway is mountainous, with top-of-the-world waterfalls.

Helsinki, the capital of Finland, borders Russia on the east and Estonia, a small border country that sits next to its neighbor, Russia, from which they became independent in 1917. The Orthodox Uspenski Cathedral, with its onion-shaped dome of Russian influence, was rather drab, but inside was an impressive display of icons. The Finnish sauna was a local ritual, and wooden toys were popular. Quaint—it retained the embodiment of its medieval atmosphere.

Estonia, with Tallinn as its capital, was one time under Danish and Swedish empires, incorporated unto the USSR after German occupation in World War II, and then, through the collapse of the USSR in 1991, became free.

Belgium, 1982

Belgium was, unfortunately, a quick pass-through. But not before appreciating Antwerp, its capital, and Brussels, all its worldly accents of international flavors and meetings.

Amsterdam, 1982

Amsterdam is part of the Netherlands, a below-sea-level country, mostly built of dikes and reclaimed land. A unique, attractive, and astonishing land renowned for its windmills and unbelievable tulip agriculture, with every color, acre after acre. Great museums: Van Gogh Museum, Rijksmuseum, and the Anne Frank House, which was popular of World War II vintage and where the family hid two years from the Nazis before they were captured. A paradise of a special way of life using canals, bridges, narrow streets, bicycles, and of course, windmills. It seemed to be currently a young people's attraction.

Spain, October 1982 to September 1983

Spain's history consisted of Phoenicians, Romans, Germanic tribes, and, probably the greatest impact, Islamic Moors. William and Arlyne had made reservations at several of the Paradores, which were national hotels with historical backgrounds and were throughout Spain. This was a wondrous way to experience Spain and its history.

Spain is Europe's second most mountainous country. Switzerland has a higher terrain; however, Spain has the Pyrenees Mountains extending from Barcelona to the Sierra Madre and goes above Granada in the south.

Madrid, the capital, boasts of the Royal Palace, Puerta del Sol, Plaza España, and the Prado; Toledo, thirteenth-century Gothic Cathedral and La Mancha (Cordoba); Seville, Palace and Alcazar and Christopher Columbus tomb; and Salamanca, Shrine of Fatima, Basilica of Our Lady of the Rosary, Baroque Plaza Mayor, El Escorial (monastery), and Palace of Philip II (1557). Barcelona was a must-see; and enjoy Les Rambles, which was partially for pedestrian and great for shopping and entertainment. The architecture was quite unique and interesting. Three separate visits didn't seem enough.

Again, adios!

Athens, 1983

Athens is the largest city and capital of Greece and one of the oldest cities in the world. Of course, its ancestral history of our civilization can claim it to be responsible for impacting and reaching so many. The invention of democracy as a form of government of the people as a center for learning in about 500 BC. It is named for the godfather of wisdom and of warfare.

The first Olympics was held in 776 BC, in Olympia, Peloponnese, not Athens. Theater was historically a prominent tradition; hence, there are 148 theater stages. A popular historic destination in the Parthenon is the Acropolis. A sacred temple atop a distant hill has been used for munitions, a church, a mosque, and Army barracks. Thus, it resulted in many archeological finds and architectural styles. Hotel Grande Bretagna, once a royal guesthouse, was used as Nazi headquarters during World War II. The changing of the guard was spectacular for the regal and colorful uniforms. Snow on the surrounding mountains made it a cold visit. They journeyed four hours south toward Poros and Piraeus, both southern port cities where William had past naval visits. Piraeus is the home of Greece's largest fleet of ships. Onward to the exciting prospect of the Greek Islands.

Greek Islands, 1983

Boarding the ship *Zeus V* at Poros, Mediterranean Sea, for seven days at the behest of Elderhostel, they were anticipating much history. The first island was Spetses, close to the mainland of Peloponnese. The lemon-egg soup and pink caviar were memorable. Next was Mycenae and the tomb of Agamemnon and the Citadel of 1500 BC.

Bronze tools here, not iron. The Lion Gate entrance of 1600 BC led to the beehive tomb, which contained eight women, nine men, plus children found covered with gold.

Epidureus belonged to Greece in 400 BC and was a home to doctors, cures, Hippocrates, Medusa, and a useful snake pit. The theater here was built in 400 BC, is still used, holds fifteen thousand to sixteen thousand people, and is known for its great acoustics.

Sparti (Sparta): They traveled through tremendous mountains and much snow, but there were few inhabitants at three-thousand-feet altitude.

Myestro is a Byzantine town five kilometers from Sparti, with cathedrals and fortresses all built on the sides of mountains and remaining houses built in 1200 BC.

Monemassia is a walled city also on the side of a mountain coming down to the sea. It was built about 1200 BC and was occupied by Phoenicians and Turks through invasion.

Hydra is a picturesque island with mules and cats.

Aegina has the Temple of Aphaia from 490 BC. Aegina disappeared, running through the forest away from Theseus. The Temples of Poseidon and Apollo were impressive.

Ephesus is an ancient port city and trade center of 10 BC. It has skeletal ruins and remains of a public library, pebble streets, and huge gymnasium; and it is the home of early Christianity. Nearby is the home of Mary and Saint John and was home to Saint Paul. Outstanding and impressive, a never-to-be-forgotten sight.

They docked at Piraeus and tried to find the sites where William docked forty years ago but, alas, were not successful.

These were all quite interesting sojourns, but life aboard the *Zeus V* was entirely a different matter. Food was mediocre, the captain and sailors performed some Greek dancing, but at the onset, the cabin assignment was not the deck cabin that had been promised. William and Arlyne were ushered to a ladder in order to descend to the hold of the ship. There was no heat, and it was a floating iceberg. There could never be enough blankets to keep you warm.

They had considered leaving the rest of the trip and debarking at the next shore opportunity but then decided that would be much too complicated. The present situation was absolutely impossible, and the chances of sleeping were nil. William was up and about the quarters they were assigned—the frozen locker—and took every imaginable measurement. He drew a plan of this dungeon too. The *Zeus V* docked and passengers debarked on March 13, 1983.

William was inwardly riled at such treatment aboard the *Zeus V* and wrote a letter to Elderhostel upon their return to the USA. He documented the trip and produced drawings and measurements of the "accommodations." His Navy engineering background clearly stressed the lack of accommodations and the many fire hazards. After all, he was a Navy captain.

The Elderhostel refunded their entire payment, which William returned with the instructions for the money to be used by someone who couldn't afford a trip with them.

Exclamation mark to this journey: On April 1983, *Zeus V* completely burned at sea, and passengers had to be evacuated. This was only a month after William and Arlyne debarked. Another blessing.

China, 1984

Beijing (Peking) was an experience not to be believed but to be endured. Richard Nixon had recently visited this "closed" country and made it open for the first time in many eons. It was a backward country with minimal living conditions, both physical and mental. Nine million in population with three thousand vehicles (but the masses were not allowed to own cars). They had horse-drawn drays, ice cream stands with blankets covering the popsicles, and billboards showing a child standing under the numeral 1. They had an all-volunteer Army where girls volunteered for three years and retired, but if promoted, they could stay. Girls could not dance in public or go into hotels, and small children wore pants with a split in the rear. Mao Tse-tung Memorial was in a huge, open square area.

William and Arlyne stayed in a hotel, Friendship, built by Russians after World War II. It had two thousand rooms, which were the pits. Beds were like rocks, sinks with constant rain leaks, and cockroaches; thermos jugs of water were delivered to the room—

one potable water and one thermos of hot water, plus tea bags and cups. An associate traveler had a bathroom that developed a leak that sprayed all over. She had to use an umbrella to use the bathroom. Forbidden City has the National Peace Museum built in AD 1400, and until AD 1911, "people" were not allowed in.

Shanghai

They visited the number three hospital, and acupuncture was performed for William and Arlyne; they visited the ICU and CCU, and everything was fifty years behind the times. HI (government) department store was extremely dirty, the living conditions were atrocious, and people stopped to stare right in your face. Foreigners were an anomaly. They flew from Nanking to Beijing, which took one hour and twenty minutes.

Nanking

It was not as dirty as Shanghai. They stayed at the British Embassy Hotel, visited the palace of former Madame Chiang Kai-shek and lunched there. There were more bicycles than Shanghai. They visited Sun Yat-sen's tomb atop a zillion steps. A Chinese couple asked for a photo of their young daughter, wife, and Arlyne, and then offered cigarettes as payment. They could speak no English. Fun! It was a six-hour train trip from Nanking to Shanghai (186 miles), passing rice paddies and water buffalos.

Great Wall of China

Six thousand kilometers long, the first emperor of China connected all pieces of the walls to unite China, and it crosses eleven provinces. William and Arlyne walked a short distance on the wall. The train to Moscow from Beijing went there two to three times per month, and it took three days. Barefoot doctors had three to six months of training and provided primary care.

William and Arlyne visited the number one hospital in Peking, a Chinese commune kindergarten, the commune leaders of a sewing shop, and a dray hauling huge boxes of water chestnuts. The hospital had a ward of twenty-five to thirty patients in crank-up beds, and the pharmacy was all herbs. The 1980 data of deaths: (1) malignant tumors, (2) cerebrovascular disease, (3) heart disease, (4) respiratory disease, (5) accidents, (6) infant diseases, etc.

William and Arlyne investigated Vietnamese boat people and refugee camp. Refugees were sleeping amid all their worldly belongings, in upper and lower cots with cramped and primitive accommodations.

Other points of interest were giant pandas, the emperor's summer palace, high-rise building construction using only bamboo materials, Mao Tse-tung's tomb, and a child's playpen stroller with wheels containing six children. Most conveyances were with manpower. The US consulate was simple and not at all elaborate.

Brazil, 1985

Seeing the statue of Christ on the crest of the mountain as they approached Brazil was an inspirational, impressive, and welcoming sight to behold. Rio de Janeiro was a long air journey from New York. The shore and beach activities were popular and crowded. Destitutes, prostitutes, beggars, and pickpockets were rampant. There didn't seem to be an overwhelming feeling of welcome. The areas where precious stones prevailed was an oasis of sorts. Taking chances on restaurants became daring but, as it turned out, were actually quite well done. Nevertheless, the stay was, gratefully, short.

1985

Nevertheless, the time came for the need to sell and leave their home, the Wayside Church in Philadelphia. Exceedingly unique, this lovely 1873 nondenominational stone church was a historical Pennsylvania landmark, complete with carriage shed sans cemetery; and this was their happy, comfortable home for several years. It was painful to leave. It was impossible to describe the ambiance and the experiences that both felt was a once-in-a-lifetime experience. Business sense dictated the decision, however.

Other offices established for the businesses were in Pennsylvania and Delaware. Having contracts now in several other states, buying a house in Florida provided better positioning for an additional office. The new house would answer that need.

The new one-acre residence would also include the constant required attention of landscaping since everything grew at record speed all year in Florida. Arlyne enjoyed this responsibility, while William felt blessed not to have to deal with this requirement. Not his cup of tea.

Puerto Rico, 1985

Now close to the Florida house, the Virgin Islands and Puerto Rico appeared on the traveling agenda to visit. Both were looking forward to landing in San Juan, Puerto Rico, where they had previously made reservations to stay in the hotel El Convento, a former convent for nuns.

Some of the later special, unique, and interesting sites here were the underwater revelation of phosphorescent fish and the coffee plantation of the mountainous wonderland, El Yunque National Forest. This was a tremendously informative and a joyful experience.

Adios!

England, 1985

Following later that year was a return and working trip to London, but William and Arlyne didn't miss this opportunity for more exploration.

During this sojourn, they decided to touch base with some friends of long ago who lived in Wigan, Lancashire. This was always such enjoyment to renew their friendship and do some catching up, of course. That was always nice, but the traveling from London to Lancashire was an experience by itself. This was such a scenic and educational look into the interior parts of England and its mining areas. It was tremendously interesting to note the language variation. The challenge was to attempt to change gears for understanding; it was definitely not simple, at times, to understand English.

Nairobi, Kenya, Africa, March 13, 1985

Jomo Kenyatta is regarded as the father of the country and declared at the birth on December 13, 1963. A large statue of him reigns over the Kenyatta Mausoleum. The Mary Leakey Museum was overwhelmingly terrific. Swahili is the official language here.

The safari initial sight was a herd of twelve giraffes. They were huge and beyond belief. This was only the beginning of an outstanding several days of following animals: gazelles, giraffes, impalas, topi, hartebeests, wildebeests, zebras, warthogs, hyenas, vultures, hippopotamuses, waterbuck, jackal, ostriches, elephants, baboons, hyraxes, foxes (mostly silverbacks), cape buffalo (male herds are separate from female herds), and guinea hens. An extravaganza of the animal kingdom.

The Great Rift Valley was a tremendous sight along with the Serengeti Plain, with the huge herds of elephants. This was Africa in its unique wonderland of animal kingdoms.

Visiting the Ngulia Lodge at the Tsavo Game Reserve was unique since it was high on a volcanic mountain. The Amboseli Game Reserve was at Mount Kilimanjaro, which has an altitude of 19,340 feet; and after much patience waiting for clouds to dissipate, the snow-covered mountain was ecstatic to see. The Mount Kenya Safari Lodge and Mount Kenya Animal Orphanage were both owned by Stephanie Powers and William Holden. The orphanage housed 150-year-old turtles, ocelots, bush babies, and many other strange jungle animals. William and Arlyne were rather awed to stand on the equator here (latitude 00'00, altitude 7,000 feet).

One of the safari vans broke down in the Masai territory. Four young tribal boys with spears bargained for possessions. There was a gun in the van for protection against the Tanzanians.

Mara Sarena Lodge was an overnight stay, as the young Masai boys danced, depicting the hunt. As William and Arlyne walked back to their cabin in the evening after dinner, they saw a hippo feeding along the compound walk. They also heard lions roaring beneath their window most of the night. Masai natives were night guards, carrying spears. Not the most comforting sight in the dark.

Masai natives were vocal, expressive, goat, herders of cattle and donkey, and believed the land was holy, so they would not till the soil. The Kikuyu tribes, by comparison, were stoic, gentle, and peaceable. The Masai villages were built in a circle; the homes were framed with twigs and small branches and, lastly, covered with cow dung. The men might have fine wines, and wives were required to build their own houses. Both men and women wore bright cloths or blankets, usually red or orange, wrapped around their bodies. Most all had shaved heads.

The women carried huge loads on their backs or heads, perhaps a child in a sling in front, and were barefoot. Ears were the targets for beauty—elongated, bejeweled, and with various-shaped holes.

The Masai were the least culturalized. They believed that if you took their pictures, you were taking their souls. Safari usually began at 5:30 a.m., returning to the lodge for breakfast at 9:30 a.m. The second run of the day was from 3:30 p.m. to 7:30 p.m. Lions galore, wildebeest by the hundreds, large herds of elephants, and the ugly marabou were seemingly plentiful. Late at night, it was exciting to watch a waterhole and the visiting animals. One that was quite special happened to be at Loitokitok but very near to the Tanzanian border, which made it a little tense.

It was a little difficult for those living in remote areas to have any hospital or medical access. William and Arlyne toured one such facility in the bush where the flying doctors come to assist. At Kijabe Hospital, the operating room was approximately eight by eight feet, containing one litter, one cabinet, and no running water. Patients were in antiquated beds next to open, screenless windows. The dead were placed outside in the hyena paths.

Other hospitals visited had 126 beds with a census of 200. They slept two in a bed if needed.

This was an incredible, enjoyable, and outstanding journey. It was tremendously educational too. A huge opportunity to appreciate comparisons.

Hawaii, 1988

There were so many separate islands of interest, but certainly, the island of Oahu was the best for William and Arlyne. Some of the best-known Hawaiian highlights were the leis, a lovely ring of flowers placed around your neck to greet you; whale watching; the Dole pineapple cannery; and the Diamond Head at Waikiki Beach. Mauna Loa is the largest and the highest volcano (land form) in the world at 4,500 feet above sea level and 13,000 feet below sea level; and it had the longest eruption. This was the home of the goddess Pele, the volcano goddess of fire, whose home was Halemaumau.

Kilauea became their favorite. To watch a live volcano roll out the molten lava and roll down all aglow and empty, still steaming, into the water was an experienced to be remembered forever. They observed an entire town struggling to abandon their homes, having been in the path of the fire producing lava. Kilauea was 60 feet wide, had eruptions lasting 12 hours every 3 to 4 weeks, and produced 700-foot to 1,300-foot-high lava at 2,100°F. There were cracks in the surrounding earth emitting steam. Roads became impassible in many directions. Aa is shredded pahoehoe or shiny lava, and when lava rolls into the ocean, it creates underwater pillows. Unusual were the black sand beaches made from the lava going into the ocean.

Maui

Maui and Kauai (Garden Island), which is the oldest island, are two other popular islands with sugar cane fields and mountains.

Oahu is home to the World War II Memorial, commemorating the resulting bombings and high number of deaths. This island had problems with feral pigs, goats, rats, and cats. Nene (ducks) were provided protection by the mongoose and had evolved from the

Canadian goose. Hawaiian Royal Palace (1882–1893) was the last of the monarchs of Hawaii.

Alaska, 1989

Before heading to Alaska, William couldn't resist the allure and enticement of Oregon's John Day River rafting. Equipped with an overnight tent and appropriate attire, this journey took on a greatly unexpected event.

They had been advised at the outset that a small group was ahead of them by two days and that one member had drowned and was not yet found.

Overwhelmed with the excitement of first-time river rafting, it was all-hands-on-deck. It was great fun until they came to a river area of calm. Arlyne was perched at the aft end of the boat, which gave a constant appreciative view of the area as they went; then with a quickening pulse and an octave-higher voice, she screamed, "There's a body floating at starboard!"

The two guides of the party swiftly paddled the boat to shore and off-loaded the passengers. In seconds, the guides had wrapped the body and brought the body of a sixteen-year-old boy to shore. Securing and covering the body, the guide called ahead for support while the passengers stood transfixed by this unreal nightmare.

Later that evening, all passengers had been transported to the predetermined shore and landing, had put up their tents (home away from home for the night), and sipped hot chocolate at the shore fireside. It was dusk, the water was lazily passing through, and the sun was almost gone when a small boat, containing the covered body of a sixteen-year-old boy, quietly made its way downstream. The silence was deafening. Blessings to everyone, please.

Onward to Vancouver and Alaska. The glorious flower gardens of Vancouver, Canada, were beyond spectacular. William and Arlyne needed that marvelous affirmation of joy and living.

The cruise would always be remembered for the tremendous number of bald eagles that continued to live both sides of the waterways. The icebergs were numerous, some with a few polar bears play-fully enjoying themselves.

The various towns they visited were Russian architecture with the onion domes that were simply but strongly built. A few places they visited were Malaspina, Ketchikan, Juneau, Sitka, Fairbanks, and Glacier Bay. Alaska is the largest of all fifty states, being two and a half times the size of Texas. Imagine, it would reach from coast to coast of the US mainland or cover eight states in Central US and has more coastline than all the US. Ketchikan has thirteen feet of rain per year and last year had eight days of sunshine.

How do we get to Florida?

Jerusalem, 1993

Arriving in Jerusalem in 1993 was instantly an experience William and Arlyne would never forget. The Ben Gurion Airport had commendable high security and understandably so. Residence to cover their scheduled time was at the Hebrew University, Mount Scopus. This was situated next to the Mount of Olives and afforded a magnificent view of the walled city of Old City Jerusalem, especially at night.

The Mount of Olives was the site where Jesus spent his final days and encompasses the Tomb of Mary at the Garden of Gethsemane. Eight of these olive trees were said to have seen the days of Jesus. Other various sites of profound interest were the Knesset, the home of Israel's government; Hasidic Jewish Quarters, which were quite restricted; Windmill, which ground flour; and housing problems, which they observed. The size of Israel in 1967 was about the size of New Jersey. The Six-Day War added 10,260 square miles in 1967. One could drive in Israel from north to south in one and half hours, and from east to west in fifty minutes.

The Old City, Jerusalem, is divided into four quarters: Armenian at the southwest corner; Jewish at the southeast corner; Christian at the northwest corner; and Muslim at the northeast corner. The Armenian Quarter boasts the ornate and beautiful church of the Cathedral of Saint James. The Muslim Quarter is the home of the

Dome of the Rock (aka El Aksa Mosque), built in AD 691, which was the rock on which Abraham prepared to sacrifice his son Isaac (Ishmael to Muslims) to prove his loyalty to God.

The Shuk was the Jewish shopping alleys of the Old City. While shopping at the Shuk, William passed a Muslim salesman who grumbled, "You going to wait and buy from the Jews?"

Oy gevalt!

Yad Vashem is the Holocaust Memorial. There were many soldiers and police along the way since they found an Israeli soldier killed the day before. There was a funeral on March 16, 1993—a very tense time. Other places of interest were Billy Rose Memorial Gardens, Israel Museum, Dead Sea Scrolls found in Qumran 1963 (from AD 68), and Parliament buildings. The oldest known map of Jerusalem was a mosaic in the wall of the Old City and was truly fascinating.

The holy month for Muslims is Ramadan, when over two hundred thousand Muslims celebrated via the call to prayer over the loudspeakers five times a day—the only sound in all Jerusalem. Other areas of profound interest: Jaffa (Tel Aviv), a port city that Napoleon destroyed in 1799 and was later rebuilt by the Turks; Mount Zion, a tomb of King David, room of the Last Supper, and house of Caiaphas; Bethlehem, where the Basilica of the Nativity was; and at a lower level, built by Constantine, was the Grotto of the Nativity.

Herod rebuilt the temple in 34–4 BC and his palace at Masada. The Wailing Wall was the last acting wall of the temple and the only remnant to survive Roman destruction in AD 70 and where only men were allowed. Women were allowed to be in the back of a metal barrier. Prayers were written on small pieces of paper and tucked into the cracks of the wall.

Shalom!

Egypt, 1993

Recognizing Cairo as an historic embodiment of multitudinous ancient artifacts made it an overwhelming and exciting introduction to Egypt. They had reservations at Mohammed Ab Palace, to which William gave a C-. Surprisingly, great breakfasts, however.

While attending the American University as students, it produced a great appreciation of the valuable lectures on culture up to Egypt today. The general impression was one of an overcrowded city of pathetic squalor, was not at all sanitized, but had many police usually in squads.

Cairo had cardboard cities where people had built their homes, hundreds and thousands of them, out of cardboard or with whatever they could find. Overpopulation was a megaproblem. City of the Dead is a cemetery where people actually lived among the dead and was amazing. Shack-like, temporary-looking rooms had been built atop other stable buildings. Pollution was extremely bad, with goats, camels, and donkey carts a part of the city traffic.

William and Arlyne visited the gigantic pyramids of Giza, which were extremely close to the city of Cairo, and they rode camels. They also toured the inside of a small area of a pyramid. More than ninety-five pyramids were constructed and were still in existence.

The Cairo Museum was only a block away from the American University, and one day was scheduled for a visit to the museum. What a wondrous, wondrous day and so overwhelming, with an overload to absorb. William and Arlyne skipped a day of school to revisit the Museum. All-encompassing were King Tut's treasures discovered in 1922.

King Tut became king (pharaoh) when he was six years of age, and he was nineteen years old when he died. His death was attributed to an inherited malady, and he walked with a cane. The treasures were overflowing in the tombs of chariots, chairs, necklaces, rings, milk, beer in urns, plus other treasures tucked in his neck bandages. It was beyond comprehension to observe or to describe the Sphinx up close.

The following week, a German tourist bus that was parked in front of the museum was bombed. Grateful to be out of harm's way, William and Arlyne had a domestic flight from Cairo Airport to Isis Hotel in Luxor, the capital of Thebes.

Luxor, Egypt, 1993

A buggy ride along the Nile River in Luxor brought them time to breathe deeply once again. The ferry transported them to the West Bank and the Valley of the Kings. There were sixty-two tombs there and many yet to be discovered.

The Valley of the Kings was far beyond overwhelming. The Temple of Karnak was incredibly stupendous, with all its many temples covering over two hundred acres, which was built in 2000 BC. Most important was the largest Temple of Amun Ra. This is the largest temple in the world. Most kings and dynasties added their buildings, gates, sanctuaries, and small chapels as time passed. It was difficult to understand and absorb because of its immensity.

Here was the Citadel of Saladin, who was husband to the Queen of Sheba. Also, here was the Temple of Queen Hatshepsut (2135–2040 BC), who was a queen dressed like a man and told the story of her father being the god Ra.

Much of this history emanated from 9500 BC, and William and Arlyne were greatly impressed with all the archaeology and the promise of so much more to come.

Returning to Cairo Airport, there was tremendous security everywhere, which included four separate security checks before boarding the plane.

Queen Elizabeth II, 1993

Cunard's cruise liner *Queen Elizabeth II* (*QEII*) was heading for a five-day cruise from New York to Southampton, London, on October 1, 1993. William and Arlyne were anticipating a five-day, five-star vacation. The ship was beautifully appointed in all ways, including fabulous meals and great entertainment. About three days out to sea, and all this particular enjoyment assumed a monstrously negative aura. Breakfast was, assuredly, first class, including a beautifully set round table for four in the breakfast room. A lovely atmosphere in this elegant room, equivalent to a thirteenth floor of a building. Suddenly, with no warning, all this ambience turned into panicsville. This huge ship was turned over on its side, and furniture, glassware, and people were thrown in every direction. William and Arlyne went belly flop across the top of the table and hung tightly to the other side. Meanwhile, one of the table's occupants was seen still in her chair, traveling swiftly backward until she hit a serving station. It all happened so quickly, and it was bedlam in every direction.

What was later described as a rogue wave, thirty feet high, was breaking on the windows of the "thirteenth-floor" restaurant. The wave broadsided the ship into a deep roll, described as a big hill.

From the *London Times*:

> Passengers were thrown across the dining room. Glasses were broken and a grand piano skated across the dance floor and back again after breaking free from its metal fixtures.
>
> People were hanging on when it suddenly rolled back to starboard and kept going.

The admiral used the public address system to ask all passengers who could make it to gather in the Queen's Lounge. After stepping over people and trying to avoid smashed glass everywhere, William and Arlyne reached the Queen's Lounge. They sat on a weighted large, brown leather sofa, and William left to go to the restroom. Arlyne was sitting alone on this huge sofa when a second rogue wave arrived. Arlyne was swung in a large half circle but remained on the sofa. This wave was very forceful but did not compare to the first wave, thank God. Where was that cup of tea that fixed everything? Despite the confidence of the admiral's announcement to the passengers, the future didn't look all that positive: "Be assured the *QEII* was built for the North Atlantic and is a safe ship."

Everything on board was, indeed, affected; the casinos were damaged beyond repair, musicians were hunting instruments and their sheet music, and all entertainment ended. The dancers couldn't be sure where the floor would be at any time. Best not to know about food details. Not a *Titanic* but a nightmare to be sure. The ship continued through rough seas, and sleep was not at all restful.

When the ship docked at Southampton, England, there were many ambulances waiting. Broken bones and injuries were multitudinous but, thank God, no deaths. A huge ship turned over on its side while you were a passenger was not taken in stride.

Bon voyage!

Concorde (Paris Orly Airport), 1994

Excitement for this journey on the Concorde could never be put into words. This was going to be the thrill of a lifetime—Paris, France, in three hours from New York. After breakfast at the Hilton Hotel (New York City), William and Arlyne were transported to JFK International Airport.

After boarding the Concorde, settling back into the shoulder-to-shoulder seat, and while sipping champagne, takeoff was as scheduled. The well-pressurized cabin was perfect, and a digital Machmeter allowed them to follow the speed and altitude (four Rolls-Royce 593 engines). Altitude was to be 56,000 feet, soaring at cruising altitude of 11 miles above earth and moving at a speed of Mach 2—twice the speed of sound is expected. Paris was only three hours away. Really?

William and Arlyne were already enjoying a delightful and very special meal approximately one hour after takeoff, and the first pilot spoke to the cabin, "We are having a bit of a problem."

In essence, he was conveying there was a difficulty in not being able to open one of the engine doors. This description was definitely nontechnical, but basically, it meant JFK control tower was to make the decision to either abort the flight and return to JFK or to continue to Paris. This meant adding another hour since they could not maintain altitude, meanwhile considering the thought of perhaps what they were not sharing.

Finally, the pilot informed the passengers that the flight had to return to JFK. This presented some real complications. The Concorde did not usually land with much fuel on board and, at the same time, was restricted from dumping fuel overboard at sea.

Landing at JFK was more than breathtaking. Landing with unfathomable speed, William and Arlyne were sure they would never stop before coming to Philadelphia. However, amid fire engines and ambulances already awaiting the arrival, all came safely to a thankful stop. It was an impossible feat, landing at extraordinary speed.

Next decision after being ushered to a plush waiting room containing everything possible to make one comfortable and a three-hour wait, the Concorde problem would be supposedly (and assuredly) corrected.

They again boarded the plane and, three hours later, landed at Orly Airport, Paris. Dollars and cents-wise, they experienced two takeoffs and two landings, instead of one of each, if you want to look at the positive side. Retrospectively, they were relieved to land at Orly. One such ride was enough, and that was a positive viewpoint.

Adieu!

Italy, 1996

Although William and Arlyne had had stops previously in Italy over the years, this particular trip was devoted strictly to vacationing and exploration.

Siena, in Northern Tuscany, Italy, was of exceptional enjoyment, not only for the welcomed serenity of the countryside but the beautiful, important, and medieval city, which was wonderfully unchanged. It was rich in history, and Chianti vineyards were nearby to visit.

Semiannually, the Palio horse races presented horse racing competition within the Piazza del Campo. They imported all the dirt for the dirt track on these occasions. Pre- and post-parades strutted through the narrow streets, carrying more flags than one had ever seen, and natives performed while robed in medieval costumes. This was a production for everyone's amazement and never to be forgotten. William and Arlyne adored Siena and held it as wonderfully special.

Having had three previous trips to Venice, William and Arlyne had already seen all the obvious tourist sites. They decided to roam the nontourist backstreet areas. Absolutely vacated and stillness prevailed, they lazily spent time enjoying the quaint arched little stone walking bridges everywhere necessary to cross the waterways.

While they were draped over the edge of one such bridge, a gondola quietly appeared, holding two persons lying within, and was beneath the bridge where they stood. The smiling couple within the gondola were looking up at William and Arlyne with rather expectant smiles, especially the male. As they were passing, Arlyne said to him, "You look familiar."

And William, at Arlyne's elbow, instantly interjected, "You look like my brother!"

The male quickly responded with a huge grin, "I am your brother."

And the gondola disappeared underneath the bridge. It was John Ritter of TV's *Three's Company*. And William never had a brother or a sister.

Florence, with its renowned statue of Michelangelo's David, is in Central Italy. Uffizi Gallery had works collected by the Medici family; Duomo Cathedral; and Palazzo Vecchio, a palace from the thirteenth century were only some of the enormous number of landmarks and fascinating history that faced one at every turn. Driving south toward Rome, there were some small fortressed towns, complete with flags of hammer and sickle insignia of the Red Communists. Milano and its enthralling Cathedral and Opera House were not to be ignored.

Vatican City, farther south, would take several days alone to do justice to all the Vatican's treasures and history. The immensity of the city; the Sistine Chapel and Michelangelo's offering; the sacred tombs, especially Saint Peter's; the statues; the Swiss Guards; and so much more to experience and to internalize the depth of these treasures. William was entirely transported into another time zone and loved it. Arlyne was deeply impressed and appreciated the reality of their presence, but it didn't equal William's enchantment.

While entering Rome in their little, green rental car, William observed rather tartly and questioned, "Are all vehicles in Italy painted a vomit green?"

However, they made a big mistake in deciding to turn in their rental car, rationalizing that because Rome was the traffic hub of all life forms, it would be better to depend on taxis. Wrong!

Having waved down the first taxi and feeling fortunate about that and having the availability of suitcases stacked inside. They had traveled approximately two city blocks when this entire communistic country went on strike. The entire country. Everything, every vehicle, just everything stopped where it was. Period. What to do? They had no choice. They got out of the taxi, with suitcases in tow, and looked for their hotel. Stranded in busy Central Rome. Now what does one do, who is a foreigner and not familiar with the entire environment, dragging suitcases? You get out and start walking.

However, all this did not detract from the zillion of wonders to behold, such as the Colosseum, catacombs, the Trevi Fountain, the Spanish Stairs, and the building called the Wedding Cake. Roller skates would be advantageous.

Arrivederci!

Monaco, Nice, Paris, France, 1996

Paris: Having spent time in Germany and having close friends living in Paris, William and Arlyne made several trips to Paris. The restaurants were, of course, outstanding, but unfortunately, experiences with all the marvelous tourist attractions almost became mundane. What a shame. Nevertheless, the Moulin Rouge, Notre Dame, Rue de la Pas, Opera House, Versailles, Eiffel Tower, Louvre, Arc de Triomphe, Montmartre, Napoleon's Tomb, and the Seine River would all remain in a special place in their memories.

Nice and Monaco: A trip farther south to Nice was a rather happy trip, with an incidental trip to Monaco. Monaco was impressive in its rather miniscule entirety. Although quaint, the palace, high on a hill, was picturesque and breathtaking. A visit to the casino completed a satisfied wonderment.

Majorca and Capri were unique, interesting, and surprising islands in their presentations.

Summary

Some of these countries were visited more than once for various reasons, including two people's profound need to satisfy curiosity, the joy of exploration, and the reveling in absorbing a wealth of education. This, in all reality, epitomized the status quo for this exceptional couple.

Of course, what would traveling be if it did not include exploring and visiting the United States of America, a country of great expectations? With the exception of nine states, the remaining states were visited, respected, appreciated, and loved.

Although William had been strongly encouraged years ago to earn his admiralty status in the Navy, business and travel took precedence. He never looked back even though he always carried his love for the Navy in his heart. The flying bridge, the topmost part of the ship, was the meaningful emblem for him to always strive to seek the top and to be the best you can be.

Salute the flying bridge!

Full speed ahead.

4

Not a Burden but an Opportunity

The nineties became the introduction into new territories, business-wise and country-wise. Finally, the businesses were sold. This implied that much national traveling waned, and gratefully so, but international travel did not seem to diminish.

William continued his daily running, and they both loved dancing, so that took care of the exercise requirement. Loving the arts, satisfying their inner need to do for others, and taking time to adore the winter sunsets across the lake each day all gave momentum and graded importance.

Arlyne was now also keeping a weather eye on William's overall behavior for any departures. She must also consider that insight into William's personality wasn't always representative of the polite, gracious, and genteel gentleman who usually predominated in business and elsewhere. Actually, with all his experienced savoir faire, he maintained little to no self-involvement with most people, and then that was on a short-term basis. Any social situation that displeased him, he would gracefully exit.

Guests not of his interest, he would, albeit quietly, leave the room and not return. Usually, he would go to the bedroom for a nap. If asked for a reason, it would be because he valued his time. Indeed! On most occasions, his sense of humor always on tap allowed him to draw people into his circle and, with gentility, to withdraw from unlikeable situations.

His philosophy "For the most part, people take life too seriously" surely didn't allow for the times when you must take life seriously, and there were those times. Nevertheless, he had a depth of understanding for people on all levels and was quite self-introspective.

William's self-evaluation, 1990

The following is information containing a comprehensive, efficient, self-introspection, and examination written by William in 1990. It provided Arlyne with a treasure of valuable evaluations not found until mid-1991. This was an extraordinary opportunity to address so many unspoken problems and concerns William had been inwardly feeling and not sharing.

1990 Present Problems

- dizzy for two days, to the extent of having to stay in bed for two days,
- took *antwerk* (sic) prescribed by a GP,
- sense of balance has been poor ever since,
- if I move my head too fast or put my head down, I have a wave of dizziness for 1–2 minutes,
- difficult to cope, dealing with two or more things at the same time. I start to feel confused.

Additional problems

- my ability to recall has diminished markedly, recently, e.g., does stamp go on right or left side of envelope,
- brief inability to recall the name of my cat (1–2 min) that we have had for 7–8 years,

- brief inability to remember the name of Michael Jordan (this is like forgetting the name of the President).

January 9, 1991 [William was now sixty-three years of age and was not verbally sharing these health concerns. Instead, they were inwardly contained, and he had written additional notes in detail.]

Poor Thinking

- wrong place settings (knives and forks),
- inviting O'Steens to dinner at Murphy's Restaurant (I thought O'S stood for LJS—Larry Sullivan)
- maybe transposing letters and numbers,
- forgot several times which section of my teeth I had brushed,
- parked my car and put four quarters in the wrong meter (two side-by-side meters) and put the money in the meter farthest from the car (William got a ticket),
- need to think the way through the processes which were routine in the past,
- forgot my phone numbers,
- made plane reservations for the wrong day mis-reading my monthly planner,
- generally, my overall coordination is decreasing,
- I have knocked my glasses off my head several times by walking too close to a door opening a cabinet. I've not gotten hurt, but almost took my nose off,
- my reactive responses are beginning to sputter (falter),
- I can usually think my way through processes,
- I routinely forget the day and date to compensate I wear a calendar watch,

- forgot how to turn on the car air-conditioner. It took me 25 minutes to figure out all the while being uncomfortably warm. I have started the A/C about 80–100 times. You need to press the button with "A/C" imprinted on it,
- banged my forehead on front of refrigerator. How could I have done that?
- bumped into glass patio door (poor balance).

March 5, 1991

Traveling did continue in early nineties, to Jerusalem and Egypt, sailing in the Cunard's *Queen Elizabeth II* and flying in the Concorde, when some health annoyances of William's began, subtly, to surface.

May 5, 1991

While waiting in the Newark Airport for their flight, William became uneasy and agitated. They missed their flight, and he was ambulanced to Saint Elizabeth's in Newark, New Jersey, and was given medication for atrial fibrillation (A-fib). Medicines, prescribed later, were Cardizem, Quinaglute, and Lanoxin. Arlyne wondered if this had been some kind of wake-up call for her to be more aware because he was not a complainer.

July 6, 1992

William was taken to the emergency room at the hometown hospital. At 5:00 p.m., his pulse was 157, and he was given an injection of digitalis. Dr. Gibsen contacted Dr. Pincek, and he gave a prescription of Lanoxin. Actually, he had been off all medicines. The next morning, at 6:00 a.m., he awoke with atrial fibrillation and a pulse of 151; and at 10:30 a.m., he went to Florida Hospital. Another injection of digitalis. Dr. Lanahan prescribed Norpace. After reading the medical directional insert, William decided not to take it.

August 14, 1992

At 6:00 a.m., his pulse was 112; he sat still for a few hours, and it subsided.

August 19, 1992

At 3:15 a.m., his pulse was 160.

August 28, 1992

At 1:55 a.m., he complained of a flutter in his chest; he had a pulse of 155.

At 7:30 a.m., he walked to the bathroom and had a pulse of 170; he lay down, and his pulse was 95.

At 9:00 a.m., his cardiologist was called for an appointment.

In the back of her mind, Arlyne was now wondering if they weren't spinning their wheels and what to do about it.

September 2, 1992

He was sent to Shands Hospital in Gainesville for cardio evaluation with Dr. Paula Reese.

September 10, 1992

A Holter monitor was prescribed.

September 14, 1992

He returned to Shands for an evaluation report, which was good. He took digoxin, one per day, and stopped procainamide.

October 2, 1992

He returned to Dr. Reese and received a good evaluation.

So much for the medical interruption, and the traveling continued. However, this experience did not disappear and only brought Arlyne and William a further envied closeness, understanding, and regard for each other that were undeniably exceptional. Arlyne recognized their special love, emphasized sometimes by the extremes of ordinary living, which had been tested many times, and this brought strength and blessing to their union. After all, who else would put a few selected rocks, gathered from his run, and place them lovingly on her pillow. Their health, both mental and physical, she knew, was a product of their reliant faith, plus routine regard and observations of health awareness and needs. So much for their blessings, but Arlyne was invariably and continually questioning the status of William's health. What should be planned for the future and the proper handling of these mountainous but not insurmountable questions that, perhaps, loomed ahead.

October 12, 1992

To her great consternation and surprise, Arlyne found these notes written by William and was initially alarmed until she resolved not to say anything about them for the present. William continued to have reasonable responses, no complaints, and the same sense of humor (e.g., when receiving a card for a birthday or other occasion, he would make a great act of shaking the card for money to drop out). She felt assured, nevertheless, that there were some difficulties affecting daily activities. Related to this concern, he was having vision problems, including seeing wavy lines occasionally. The neurologist said they were ministrokes. William said he had had them two to three years earlier. The recommendation was aspirin, one per day.

April 4, 1993

Planning was underway for travel to Jerusalem, Tel Aviv, Cairo, Egypt, Luxor, Valley of the Kings, and much later in the year, boarding the Cunard Liner *Queen Elizabeth II*. They were all physically demanding trips in many different ways, but the hypnotic and intriguing expected histories in Egypt and Jerusalem were beyond imagination. They were wonderfully excited about the prospects.

The resulting experience of the *QEII* rogue waves did not seem to have any depth of reaction to William, as Arlyne inwardly observed. Considering all the might-have-beens, the *QEII* fared well, with little damage on the outside of the ship, but much damage occurred throughout the inside of the ship. Passengers who were injured numbered approximately fifty, treated on board and in Southampton hospitals. William and Arlyne were fortunate to have no injuries, but sleep became elusive and difficult for the remaining voyage due to rough seas.

March 12, 1994

Early 1994, the Concorde flight became the outstanding excitement. To arrive at Orly Airport in Paris, France, in three hours from JFK Airport in New York was an incredible concept, except William and Arlyne did not experience that the first time. It really took six hours, if you included the additional three hours of required maintenance after returning to JFK.

A midyear confession came from William that he felt he was headed for Alzheimer's, and Arlyne kept saying it was probably the medicine. However, his forgetfulness, or not remembering, seemed more noticeable within the last year. An orange-colored cat crossed the road in front of their car just a few blocks from their home. William said that reminded him of a cat out of their past, and did they once have a cat like that?

Arlyne replied, mildly explaining, "Well, OJ, our present cat looks like that, I think."

William paused a moment and said, "Oh damn!"

In the morning, probably three or four times in one hour, he would ask, "What's on the agenda for today?"

Then talking about the granddaughters, he would ask, "Now, how old is Jenna, thirteen?" No, she was fourteen.

And in a short time, he would ask, "Now, how old is Jenna, twelve?" No, she was fourteen—again and again.

Some days were worse than others. His disposition remained very good despite some frustration that he was aware of his remembering problems.

So many questions and confusion whirled in Arlyne's thinking regarding this lonesomeness of decision-making. She yearned for sources of affirmation and knowledge. To whom or what should she turn to for some answers or help to her many bothersome concerns. Prayers were her immediate source, but following was the struggle for more tangible and immediate resources.

1994

Yes, seek knowledge of the disease and know with what you are dealing. She knew that would be William's approach to any questionable experiences he was having and that would direct him to find answers through libraries, doctors, and self-analysis.

A visit to the library was not worthwhile. There was one book on Alzheimer's, *The 36-Hour Day*, which was a great book but not the first book one should read. Arlyne found that out retrospectively. Researching for specialized neurologists didn't immediately surface either.

In December, William enrolled in the Office of Clinical Studies, a research program for Alzheimer medicines. He was tested as borderline and asked to return in six months.

William was having some short-term memory problems and only occasionally some balance occurrences. Arlyne was realizing, but not consumed by, these thoughts, which she had relegated to a special place in her mind.

1995

Meanwhile, William planned their trip to Panama Canal, Acapulco, and Los Angeles. Arlyne couldn't help but regard the cruise as a restful time for William. However, he was already planning a trip to Northern Italy and south to the Vatican City. Arlyne was not upset but did document in her mind a few times a seeming weakness in walking. It was probably a little too much sun, she decided. Was it lupus-related?

1995

They went to Hyatt Grand Cypress this particular day for brunch, having invited the company of another couple to join them, and William drove. Although it was not far from their home and they had been there many, many times, he didn't know how to get there at all. Arlyne sensed his lack of confidence and attempted to gently suggest a prompt at every light and crossing, which he accepted without comment.

The rear light of their auto decided to stay lighted after the car had no engine running. William got upset with Arlyne and made a pronouncement that she had to become more responsible for things.

Accepting the situation, Arlyne replied an agreement with "You're probably right!"

He had been driving and probably thought she should be more helpful to him.

A few friends dropped by for a short hello, and William was quite welcoming. He told the story of their first overnight stay at Hyatt Grand Cypress ten years ago. He told of a fire in the middle of the night, the fire engines lined up outside, and that they watched it from their room. The real story happened to be that the entire area, including stores, hotels, etc. were without electricity for a reason they never learned, and in this outage, emergency vehicles and helicopters arrived in front of the hotel to collect a resident with cardiac problems at the hotel. No fire.

1995

They had put metal shelving in the garage because they had to dispose of a rotted shelf of compressed wood that was falling apart. William decided to get a new one and had a handyman put it together about three or four months earlier. He came home one day carrying a box of metal shelving, having totally forgotten they had already been replaced.

Following a repeat of earlier days, he asked how old their grandchild Jamie was three or four times, separated by about an hour.

The usual repeats had become daily "What's doing today?" And it would be asked at 7:00 a.m., 8:00 a.m., 10:00 a.m., 12:00 p.m., etc.

Giving this behavior serious thought, and for self-preservation, Arlyne bought an erasure board and wrote the daily schedule: Month, day, when, and where.

When he asked, she would calmly direct him, "I believe I included that on the schedule board in the hall."

It worked well at first but only intermittently after a few weeks.

Reviewing the growing list of general concerns, of dressing, of ablutions each day, of driving, and then of listing medical information was definitely increasing.

1995

Arlyne was thankful that meals and appetite were not problems. He still, as always, refused to eat the bottom of rolls and would eat only the tops. This had been a historic habit. Perhaps it might harken back to his childhood experiences or even to the flying bridge syndrome. It really harmed no one, and at this point, he would probably just respond to the concern with "Did anyone die? Then it's not serious." Good observation.

They deemed, at last, that this was a necessary step to realistically review just where they were with the multiple medical input:

On October 1995, Dr. Dreher, a neurologist, was highly recommended to Arlyne, and he recommended an MRI for William at Orlando Medical Center.

Dr. Malinde, a neuropsychologist, was visited, and a thallium scan was ordered.

Dr. Candor, a cardiologist and previous Navy doctor, examined him and said to discontinue procainamide and keep digoxin.

These particular doctors were all visited within two months to determine just what all must be considered for future direction. To Arlyne, this could easily be overwhelming, but her methodical background held fast.

Contacting Dr. Dreher was, thankfully, a visit that provided confidence. He shared that Alzheimer's disease did not have much history for support at this time, and the best there was to offer was thiamine therapy, which meant mega doses of vitamin B.

October 9, 1995

A geriatric reevaluation of William at the Orlando Regional Healthcare System by Dr. Richard Nelson stated this in part:

> The patient is a 67-year-old male with a follow-up after initial visit on 8/7/95. Has primary short-term deficits particularly in the areas of language, well-preserved coping skills, deficits in general memory and his verbal memory entirely consistent with early Alzheimer's disease. His neuropsych testing shows he is an exceptionally bright gentleman with an overall IQ score in the 99th percentile.
>
> Delayed recall was significantly impaired. There is a strong family history of Alzheimer's disease. Currently compensating for his short term memory deficits with a calendar book and reminding by his wife. The patient is currently compensating as well with contact with Alzheimer's Association and apparently doing quite well. The patient will recheck in 5 to 6 weeks for follow up of his Thiamine Therapy.

November 12, 1995

A neurological reevaluation of William at the Orlando Regional Healthcare System, Memory Disorders Clinic, by Dr. Dreher, director of neurology:

> Mr. O'Gara returned to the office today accompanied by his wife. There does appear to be some worsening of his cognitive function with him stating at times he feels "foggy". This worsening seems to be only relatively recent over the last several weeks to a month. He states he is tolerating the Thiamine well and no other factors affected (i.e. visual, headaches, gait or other symptomatology).
>
> He inquired about possibly undergoing hyperbaric oxygen treatment. This cannot be recommended at this time. Exam: overall exam seems to be stable other than some worsening of his cognitive testing concerning orientation. He could not tell the month or day of the week. A reliable diagnostic tool is not yet available concerning Alzheimer's disease (short of brain biopsy).

1995

In late 1995, Dr. Dreher discontinued thiamine therapy and began Cognex. Following that was an EEG (electroencephalogram) at Orlando Medical Center.

Problems seemed to be gradually surfacing, and Arlyne was making every effort to be understanding, kind, and patient. She found this had best results. She thought at many times if she were the one in that position and how she would want to be treated. Here was her beloved William, who had always held her by the hand, now relying on her guidance and sustenance. Of course, he was her first responsibility, always, she reaffirmed to herself.

1996

Despite all this background concern, William was still putting his best foot forward with his winsome personality. To others, he remained the same person, and most people whom he knew never guessed with what he was dealing. He was a good actor.

Travel was still on his to-do list. A Mediterranean cruise in early 1996 via Monaco, Nice, Genoa, Majorca, and Capri went quite well and was probably less of a strain on him than some earlier trips. However, there were good and bad days, but the bad days were mildly accelerating and necessitating Arlyne to be on the alert for extra thoughtfulness, consideration, and love. She quietly was aware that providing these basic items was also providing security, a definite key item and need to his behavior. The tactile approach was truly necessary and produced results, she found.

An unusual instance erupted a few weeks after they returned from the Mediterranean trip. William became upset with Arlyne, and it all began over his saying he had had one bottle of beer in a year and that he had given away a case of imported beer. Arlyne was quite a bit taken aback by the information given; he was not a beer drinker to any extent. She asked him how much he had given away, and that set him off, yelling at her, "Ten, twelve, thirteen cases. Does it matter?"

She casually stepped away toward another room, and he chased after her through the rooms with unrelenting yelling. He told her she had "too much authority around here."

That might have had some truth since she was now responsible for almost everything.

About two months earlier, he had gotten upset at her, having been frustrated over his having forgotten something. He told her in no uncertain terms then that she had to take more responsibility for things. *Now, where do I stand?* she frustratedly asked herself.

With the passage of time, the intermittent problems of not remembering became more evident and more problematic. In the evening, while watching TV, he asked Arlyne if she would like an apple. She said, "Fine."

He returned from the kitchen with an apple for himself. The next night, he asked if she would like an after-dinner drink. She said, "Yes, that would be nice."

He returned later with a drink for himself only. This had happened several times with coffee. He always made the offer in the morning and asked if she would like a cup. He proceeded to make one cup for himself.

1996

Still driving, road directions seemed to be a problem now and then for William. He stated he couldn't remember where "things" were and couldn't remember what their house looked like. This was while they were in Vancouver. He couldn't remember how to get to places or routes of well-traveled roads at home either.

He awakened at 9:00 a.m. to have his cholesterol test taken at the doctor's office. He made coffee for Arlyne, but he didn't have any. At the doctor's office, he asked if his having coffee with sugar would matter, and the doctor said it would be best not to have had it, and William came home. He hadn't had any coffee.

Another try at getting his cholesterol test taken: He washed, dressed, made Arlyne coffee, had none of the coffee, needed to comb his hair before going, and ate his cereal. Foiled again.

Spelling seemed to be somewhat of a problem lately. He was always a very good speller and now, just ordinary words were misspelled. Arlyne giving directions to get something that was in a certain place was problematic. He insisted that he wanted to get something. Arlyne gave directions, and invariably, he was not successful. It must be tremendously frustrating. Arlyne made a mental note to avoid the situation in the future.

He said one day he couldn't remember his address or telephone number, and when he went to Walmart, for instance, he would draw a map on how to get there and where his car was parked. However, he was in trouble when he couldn't find his way out of the parking lot. Credit here for thinking ahead though.

1996

They had been anxiously awaiting this visit to Dr. Dreher, who provided a summary of all the recent testing, at the Memory Clinic. It was a time for holding one's breath and hoping for good news, of course. The session included blood results, neuropsychological testing, medicines, and consultation. "Very bright, very intelligent, actually brilliant."

He showed dysfunction in the language area (hippocampus area and brain stem), showed deficit in functioning, but had mental capacity to use reasoning to cope for now (October 1995).

William admitted that certain situations were complex for him, and he got confused by them. He tried to take a smaller, bite-size information. Arlyne had noticed he retreated out of these situations and tried to subtly inveigle her to take over. One example was in Richmond, Virginia. They had just arrived, wondering where and how to use the maps, written info, etc. He got absolutely nonplussed by the requirement. A year ago, he would have tackled it easily. He said, "You will have to figure out where we are going and how to get there. I'm having a bad day."

The next morning after the previous evening and four to five rehearsals of the next day's events, the first thing he said was "What have we got planned for today?"

William seemed rather adept at finessing his lack of remembering in many situations: "Yes, I was going to say that" and "What I was going to say."

1996

The year 1996 arrived amid increasing bouts of confusion and not remembering. Arlyne did not consider these at all threatening in any way.

William made a statement, "I get confused as to directions like where the destination is and how to get there." No longer a navigator, either.

He went shopping for Christmas and stopped at several places. When he got home, he said, "You know, I can't remember where I've been."

He took the Mercedes 380SL to a garage in preparation for selling the car. He couldn't remember the price we were asking and struggled to find his way home. Arlyne was now either the driver or the copilot, where transportation was required.

He lost his attaché case.

Making the decision, finally, to buy a Lexus was a celebration. They had worked diligently over two or three days to affirm the decision. Traveling up the familiar roadway, he couldn't remember where they were going or why.

Arlyne had sore throat, cough, and nasal drip, and was quite miserable in general, so she went to bed early and continued all this misery for three days. At this point, he asked, "Do you have a cold or something? Don't you feel well?" (It really made one feel cared about, but only for a moment would she feel sorry for herself.)

Although William's disposition seemed to be holding well, this week, it was quite difficult for him not to remember so many things.

Mid-March, he had another hypoglycemic attack, resulting in being in bed most of the day and resting mostly the next day. This meant several spells of sweats, nausea, and pallor, accompanied by strange feelings over his upper torso. William had had two similar spells, lasting two separate days in January and February 1996.

March 16, 1996

March 16, at 12:30 a.m., he had chest pain, irregular heartbeat, pain going to his back, and pain in his jaws. By 5:00 a.m., they decided to go to the hospital. Tests were done, and doctors decided to keep him. Dr. Candor, the cardiologist, didn't see any heart damage but did want a stress test. It was a two-day stay.

April brought another hypoglycemic attack with the usual sweats, nausea, and paleness. In the evening, he kept going in and out of those attacks, referred to as spells.

On Easter Sunday, they went to brunch at the Hyatt Hotel, and he had a similar attack there. They quickly returned home, and William went to bed for the remainder of the day.

Dr. Candor said it was time to have a glucose tolerance test, which came back negative. A later visit and test to an endocrinologist also bore no findings. Now what?

His memory and confusion were especially difficult now. Arlyne had to write all the checks and prepare for mailing to the IRS. He said he just couldn't do it.

He awakened with a very stiff neck and headache in the back of his skull. Advil didn't help.

April 12, 1996

Dr. Dreher increased Cognex strength to 4 times a day, from 30,000 mg to 40,000 mg. William was not enthusiastic in his response to Dr. Dreher's question, "Do you think meds are helping?"

He replied hesitantly, "Yeah." Last time, he was quite enthusiastic with his response, "Oh yes!"

May 15, 1996

Spells persisted off and on all day.
There was a noticeable decrease in appetite.

June 18, 1996

He had another morning in bed with spells.

June 24, 1996

The scheduled travel plan now was for Italy. In Venice, William was in bed most of the morning, with irregular heartbeat and a spell.

Returning home, it took eight days for him to recuperate, and he was very tired, taking two naps a day, about thirty-five to forty minutes for each.

He was nauseated, had no appetite, had cramps in his legs, and was swelling in his right pubic area. He had lost eleven pounds.

Arlyne called Dr. Dreher for help. A referral to a urologist was made. Dr. Dreher stopped Cognex. Good!

July 12, 1996

The spells returned.

July 23, 1996

There were several spells today (four).

July 24, 1996

He had irregular heartbeat and took extra medication. Memory failing and instances of this continued to happen. He put a kitchen stool and haircutting material in order for Arlyne to give him a haircut before he went walking in the morning. This was a reminder of the job to be done today before going north tomorrow. Arlyne had given him a haircut last evening, after dinner. All in all, a bad day.

William asked several times, "We will be having the family here for Christmas?"

An asking statement. Never had they had the family at home for Christmas day, only for New Year's, Easter, and Thanksgiving holidays. The family remained at their homes for children's enjoyment at Christmas.

1996

A wonderfully bright spot came in, having found a highly recommended support group in Orlando presented by the Alzheimer's Association. This was so valuable and helpful to Arlyne at this point when so many new concerns had newly arrived. William benefited greatly from a dedicated Alzheimer professional at the helm, Peggy Bargmann. The Alzheimer's support group numbered approximately seven to eight people each week, and it was a group of well-educated men, lawyers, mathematicians, and administrators who were eager to be helpful. It really resulted in their helping each other with professional guidance. A thoroughly successful experience for all, engendering sharing their problems and positive thinking.

William was an asset to the group, not only for his ever-flowing sense of humor but also for his occasional depth of participation. He also adored the director, Peggy, who guided them and who quietly and calmly dispensed sage information. An outstanding experience in toto.

Meanwhile, the spouses or caregivers of these men were meeting separately and sharing their concerns with each other, also with professional guidance. It was a wonderfully positive experience depicting what to do, coping skills, responding, being aware of signals, and becoming more overall effective. A great, great source of information providing comfort and confidence.

Arlyne wondered, *Must I now become an expert?* And the answer was yes. It seemed this disease was a puzzle with many, many pieces. "It is a puzzlement!"

1996

They had been invited to a friend's beach home in Holmes, Florida. The invitation was for two days, except William had erred when he put it in his calendar book with wrong dates. Later, he didn't know where he put the car, the new car. At night, when getting ready for bed, he asked what side of the bed he slept on. Thirty-eight years on the same side.

July 29, 1996

Another red-letter day. William was diagnosed with shingles. The spells also continued, averaging about twice a month. July was an exceptional month, with four experiences of spells and still no doctor's diagnosis.

September 23, 1996

Arlyne asked William to make a copy, on the copier machine, of the IRS 1040 ES check. He came to Arlyne with his checkbook, showing he had paid June and September payments on September 13 and never told her. He told her that she must do all this and gave her his checkbook. He was having obvious feelings of it all being a downer. He said, "Just another sign of losing ground."

He was so right. This sent Arlyne also to the doldrums, but she had the support group, and perhaps, she would find direction there. The support group was a blessing for both of them.

October 5, 1996

Dr. Dreher referred William to Dr. Rick for possible Aricept research program. October was a month of three spells—going to bed with sweats, nausea, paleness, and strange inner feelings all over the chest. He slept for two hours. He became a part of the August clinical trials.

October 18, 1996

More spells at 1:30 p.m. and 9:00 p.m.

Dr. Cohen, gastroenterologist, did upper and lower GI exams because William had lost twelve pounds but found no concerns.

October 9, 1996

William put the wrong dishwasher liquid in the dishwasher last evening, and they were up until midnight cleaning up suds. This had been his job for four years, using liquid Calgon only. Upon awakening the next morning, he told Arlyne of his dream that he used the wrong dishwasher liquid and was cleaning up suds. That was no dream, dear.

He said he would run a clear load through to make sure it was okay. Arlyne, coming in from working in the garden, asked if he had run the dishwasher through, and he said, "What for? Was I supposed to?"

He spent 75 percent of this day sleeping.

How could these episodes occur and yet have many days of normalcy? Arlyne had this question and many others to take to the support group and to Dr. Dreher, the neurologist.

Despite the newly found sources of help and information, the situation remained a lonely one. This disease was surely an insidious and surreptitious thief. Her uphill work these days was definitely multiplying.

She felt her own brain was spinning. Meanwhile, William was enjoying the regular MMSE testing with Dr. Dreher. It was a game that was fun.

October 20, 1996

Recalling his dream of the previous night, he said it was all about Ship's Parts. "I hate to ask you this, but what is the present situation with Ship's Parts? How is it doing? Why didn't we sell it?"

They had closed Ship's Parts in 1993 because the Gulf War ended, and it was, consequently, the last of their contracts. The US Navy had put many ships in mothballs. This was now 1996.

October 22, 1996

This was the second time William had taken something to be repaired and had no idea where he took it or left it. The copier went on the blink, and he delivered it somewhere and didn't know where. Then he took shoes to be repaired and had no idea where that was either.

Building an addition of a garage to the house had become a one-person responsibility. Understanding the building plans was much too confusing for William. He asked Dr. Dreher, "What can I do to help myself?"

Dr. Dreher replied, "Read, read, read."

William and Arlyne were talking about the book *Primary Colors* that he was beginning to read. Arlyne added that *Blood Sport* was written with real names and places.

He said, "How could they write that about the Clintons so quickly?"

She told him they had been in the White House four years. "They have?" He further asked, "Marilyn Monroe isn't dead, right?"

They were to meet the builder for the garage at the courthouse to get permits. William was driving and didn't know how to get to the courthouse.

He said to her, "How do you prefer to go?" Slick!

November 12, 1996

Dr. Candor, the cardiologist, changed William's meds from Lanoxin to beta-blocker atenolol. He was tested for Alzheimer's Aricept research program, and Dr. Candor had stopped the heart meds; otherwise William could not have participated. Both doctors felt it was important to participate. He did.

March 13, 1997

William had written the following paper concerning his self-evaluation. This was on his office desk.

> About 1–2 years ago (maybe 3–4 years ago) WOG had 20–50 separate instances which he had ////// or \\\\\\ in front of his eyes.
>
> This was before I was aware of Alzheimer's, and obviously before I was diagnosed with Alzheimer's.
>
> I have, and have had for the last 4–5 years, tachycardia and irregular heart beats. Could these

episodes have broken plaque from my arteries
and lodged in my brain? i.e. not Alzheimer's but
rather strokes and plaque formation.

WOG is trying to find something other
than progressive Alzheimer's.

Rather, plaque accumulation from the
tachycardia, which is under control of heart meds
(Lanoxin).

But—

On the other hand the ARICEPT is helping
the memory problem!

?WOG

So many continuing examples of not remembering were occurring, almost daily. He seemed to get something, one thing, on his mind and continued on it, sometimes for a few days. He did this with his son-in-law, a financial advisor, about a wrong decision at work.

1997

Spells persisted for two days in New Orleans.

With guests in the living room at home, William proceeded to explain that the center redwood mahogany coffee table was from West Africa, and he got it when he was nineteen years old. The real story was William and Arlyne had bought this slab of redwood in California about twenty years earlier and had had it refinished to its present state. Many times, his stories had not been factually correct, but this was way off base. He had brought two mahogany end tables from West Africa at age nineteen.

March 11, 1997

A day earlier, William said he enjoyed being at Universal and that he thought he would hate standing in line. "It really wasn't bad, and I really enjoyed it."

They had not been to Universal at all.

Irregular heartbeat pulse went from 158 to 65, and he had at least two spells the day before. William asked Dr. Candor about possible myocardial infarctions, and the doctor said no because the CT scan showed nothing. The doctor sent him to Shands Hospital in Gainesville to another endocrinologist, and they could find nothing. This was totally not understandable. Not possible.

June 6, 1997

William experienced rapid and irregular heartbeat for over seven hours. Dr. Candor said to bring him to the hospital for EKG. He was admitted and was there for four days. Meds were changed three times. Arlyne offered information that she had noticed his memory spiraled downward while taking a beta-blocker. They then put him on flecainide, and he seemed to be doing well so far. Arlyne reported later that memory problems had not worsened, and she didn't think he was as confused. She felt the meds had made him worse, previously to that.

June 28, 1997

At his sister-in-law's home in Pennsylvania, William had three spells, having had three consecutive days of spells ten days earlier. His sister-in-law, an RN, became very concerned for him.

July 18, 1997

William had two consecutive days of spells and complained of a lump in his throat, a first for that. The heat he generated was tremendous. His shirt was sweat-drenched. The spells did not generally last for more than twenty minutes at a time. He looked very ill and wan, with deep circles under his eyes. He had another spell later that evening. Wasn't there any answer to alleviate these? Arlyne was nonplussed, doctors were nonplussed, and dear William was continually being drained. It had been a hair-pulling time, she lamented. Could it be a food problem?

July 20, 1997

Arlyne believed William's memory had noticeably slipped and was wondering if these spells were taking a toll on his memory too.

His roomie buddy from the USMMA called, and then he couldn't remember his buddy's name.

He had no idea where Roadhouse Grill was, a favorite restaurant where they ate often. He was confused by the menu, and Arlyne had to order for him.

He couldn't make the blood pressure machine work, having used it many times previously. Arlyne didn't have a problem with it.

Jenna, a granddaughter, had had nose surgery the previous Tuesday, and William talked about it incessantly since. "How many seventeen-year-olds have you known who had a nose job?" Then later that evening, he had asked, "Did Jenna have something done at the doctors to her leg, or arm, or something?"

He had an irregular heartbeat at noon. He hadn't taken morning meds. He couldn't find them, but they were in plain sight in the bathroom, where they were always kept. Arlyne made a mental note to keep checking more closely and to be more connected to his everyday activities.

October 17, 1997

Kindergarten reunion in Pittsburgh, Pennsylvania. Kinders observed William would occasionally and unusually become very quiet. Unlike him. He told Arlyne he had a disturbing experience. He couldn't remember what their house looked like.

December 18, 1997

William and Arlyne made a commitment of donating an endowment of $1 million to the US Merchant Marine Academy (USMMA) in 1997.

The primary purpose of this advised fund and the William and Arlyne O'Gara Scholarship Fund was to assist students to achieve higher levels of academic performance, academic improvement, and monetarily rewarding individual progress. This endowment was designated and required to be used only for midshipmen.

This scholarship was devised by William and Arlyne with the mission to honor the plebe who entered the academy, worked hard, and evidenced outstanding improvement by relating his grade point average (GPA) from the previous year and appropriate to five majors, covering second, third, and fourth years (sophomore, junior, and senior).

William and Arlyne presented these awards to the deserving midshipmen at the awards ceremony each graduation. At a special dinner for the awardees the evening before graduation and before the next day's ceremony, a midshipman stated with great joy, "This is the first time I've ever won anything."

To which, William quickly replied, "You still haven't won anything. You have earned it."

This was a yearly extremely happy event. William and Arlyne looked forward to presenting these special awards to USMMA's outstanding midshipmen who had, obviously, worked long and hard. Pure joy for all.

Carpe diem!

May 8, 1998

A very special day. It was the dedication of the William and Arlyne O'Gara Room in Wiley Hall, USMMA, Kings Point Academy, Kings Point, New York. A beautiful, stately, and formal room in what had been the Chrysler Mansion, a summer home with twenty-four rooms and ten baths, which was now called Wiley Hall.

William and Arlyne, 1998, room dedication at Wiley Hall, United States Merchant Marine Academy, Kings Point, New York

William and Arlyne, cutting the ribbon at room dedication, Wiley Hall (Chrysler Mansion), 1998, USMMA

Admiral Mattheson, Arlyne, and William O'Gara, Wiley Hall,
USMMA, Arlyne and William O'Gara Room, 1998

William and Chinese special friend, Nanking, China, 1984

Rear Admiral Thomas Matteson, superintendent, presented a grandiose introductory speech, at which time he presented Arlyne with a beautiful Seiko watch and corsage. William, as an alumnus of 1950, gave a short speech of acceptance with some main points that he summarized.

This was an event that was important, solemn, and joyous to him. He stressed that whatever accomplishments might have been in his life, he owed to the education he received at Kings Point, which was dear to his heart and held this dedication as a great honor.

He continued to clarify that this occasion represented two things profound in his heart. First was to be able to repay Kings Point in some way, and second was to show his gratitude and indebtedness to be able to promote a scholarship for the midshipmen.

He felt it a joyous event for both him and his wife to be so honored and thankful to have their names associated with such a beautiful room.

Some of his classmates and staff were present for the occasion, which, of course, added great enjoyment for William as well.

The William and Arlyne O'Gara Room's entrance has a plaque and etched in gold over the entry reads "William & Arlyne O'Gara Room." The ribbon-cutting ceremony was wonderfully enhanced by an honor guard of sharp-looking, attractive midshipmen. A large portrait of William and Arlyne adorns the left wall of the room, and a lengthy engraved plaque of an impressive biography is placed beneath the portrait. William and Arlyne were also given an exact replica of their plaque, and it hangs on the wall of their home, along with two other past wooden-engraved awards. One reads beneath the academy seal "Distinguished Service Award—William and Arlyne O'Gara, October 8, 1998." And the other reads "Distinguished Service Award, Outstanding Achievement, William O'Gara, October 5, 2000."

Facta, non verba. (Actions, not words.)

Previous to the marvelous event, however, Arlyne had, for weeks before, gently kept suggesting and nudging William to write a speech in preparation for the dedication. He had some kind of denial each time. Arlyne even offered to write one for him, and he denied that too. This was at the time that he had been also diagnosed with

Alzheimer's disease (1998). Finally, cornered on the plane and supplied with paper and pen, he wrote some reminder notes. That was somewhat of a relief for Arlyne.

When he gave the speech, he soon got the cards all mixed up and, with a dramatic gesture, crumpled the cards and threw them over his shoulder, saying, "Well, you know I have Alzheimer's!"

The admiral burst out laughing, as did most of the audience, for it was said as a joke. No, it was not a joke, but no one there knew differently. He had already been diagnosed three years at this point.

May 27, 1998

A copy of a letter from his USMMA roommate of forty-eight years ago was a highlight for William.

> May 27, 1998
>
> Dear Billy and Arlyne,
>
> I cannot express to you the honor and pride I had in you for your most generous gift to the Academy. I felt highly honored to have been your invited guest. You did me a great favor by having me included in your list of guests. It was a special moment for me that I shall treasure and remember all the days of my life.
>
> I have to say that Arlyne was and is a most strikingly beautiful woman and I am sure, wife. You both, particularly Arlyne, looked handsome and well turned out. I am completely amazed by how much you remain the same, in looks and in your little tour d'force acceptance. You were great.
>
> Enclosed are a few pictures I managed to get off during the ceremony.

Thanks a MILLION Billy Boy and Arlyne.

Sincerely yours,
Bobby Joe (O'Dwyer)

1998

Upon leaving the house on New Year's Eve, William asked if they shouldn't turn off the outside lights so the trick-or-kids won't come to the house.

February 3, 1998

William began having trouble with urinating, and at 3:00 a.m., he could not void. They drove to the emergency room upon his passing blood in the urine. He returned home with a leg bag.

April 11, 1998

A cystoscopy was performed.

June 20, 1998

He was wondering if his birthday had passed. He was looking at his Father's Day card that lay on the coffee table before him. His birthday is August 15. The family joyfully celebrated anyway.

June 22, 1998

One hour after having dinner at Shells Restaurant, they went shopping at Sam's Club. He asked Arlyne if she was hungry and if they were going for dinner at any special place.

July 22, 1998

Celebrating William's birthday, they went to Arthur's 27 Restaurant. Concepts of the menu were just too confusing for him. The bill arrived, and he added a tip. It totaled $250. He had it so terribly mixed up with doubling the amount and adding upside down and sideways.

August 26, 1998

Traveling from Philadelphia to Newark Airport, it became obvious he didn't understand the map or directions. He pulled off the road and asked Arlyne if she would figure it out. Also, later, he was driving because he wanted to drive. They were going to Mount Dora when he suddenly pulled over, stopped the car, and said he wasn't seeing the best. Perhaps it was an instinct for safety, she observed as an admired move.

August 28, 1998

On their wedding anniversary, Arlyne gave him a card he really appreciated. They talked of days and events gone by. On their way to dinner, he asked if they could stop by a store so he could get a card. Returning home from dinner, he asked when her birthday was. She softly related to him that it was a month ago, to which he groaned, "Oh no!"

And then he laughed, realizing he had it all mixed up. They made it a fun time. Arlyne lovingly admired her birthday card.

September 3, 1998

They were in Boston, staying at the Hyatt Hotel, and William had spells all day. He had showered before deciding to watch TV but then decided to read the paper. Then he showered again. Arlyne offered a nonessential observation.

"I think you showered already."

"What is that saying? A woman can't have too many?"

"Too thin or too rich." He went in the other room and returned, saying, "What is that saying? A woman can't have too many?" Then they had the same conversation over again.

"What's happening tonight? Where are we going tomorrow? Why are we here? Is Jackie Kennedy still married to Ari Onassis?"

Traveling was getting a bit overwhelming, Arlyne decided.

1998

After a somewhat lengthy discussion between William and Arlyne, they decided it was a propitious time to present their idea to the Alzheimer's Association to establish an Alzheimer's Library in Orlando. They had already experienced the initial difficulty and availability of seeking helpful material appropriate to Alzheimer's disease. They felt this could be a source of enlightenment for so many in need of this kind of information. Knowledge is power, not only for furnishing Alzheimer information but also for anyone with a related dementia, students, and healthcare professionals to cope, to grow, and to have hope. It was now the O'Gara Library at the Alzheimer's Association.

Arlyne and William at dedication of the O'Gara Library
at Alzheimer's Association, Orlando, Florida, 2000

William and Arlyne O'Gara's photo that is on the shelf in the
O'Gara Library, Alzheimer's Association, Orlando, Florida, 2000

2000

Annette Kelly, MSN, ARNP, the CEO of the Central and North Florida Chapter of the Alzheimer's Association, was the dedicated shining light of the O'Gara Library at the Alzheimer's Association and its success. It became the largest Alzheimer or dementia collection in Florida, containing books, videos, computer programs, journals, audiotapes, and activities—all at no charge.

1999

The EASE (Early Alzheimer's Support and Education) Program Support Group remained a vital part of William's weekly schedule. It was directed by Peggy Bargmann, RN, BSN, whom he especially liked and respected, as did the other members. William really enjoyed the give-and-take and also the occasional projects. The Memory Book was especially enjoyable. He supplied a collection of past photographs, which spawned special stories as he explained each photograph. A treasure.

The support group resulted in being a great addition and source of guidance. Peggy was the tremendous force to each member, and they loved her. William dubbed her "Pedgy" forever. She never lied to them, even when their questions could have indicated the opportunity. Peggy recognized that for each member, it was a very important period of acceptance of the disease. She also found that the members developed a responsibility for each other, which was very important when profound issues were broached. William was quoted as saying, "We don't want to wallow in self-pity. I have a life to live, and I intend to do just that!"

He never felt sorry for himself and never wavered from his flying bridge syndrome.

Up anchor!

In a particular support group meeting, the topic arose of when it was time to stop driving. This was, knowingly, going to be a hot topic. It did, indeed, ignite a multitude of reactions and profound attitudes from every member present. Understandably and basically, this foreshadowed a knowing cessation of their independence. Arlyne was aware this also presented a large requirement for strategy, planning, and tact for the caregiver to manipulate.

It was again a hair-pulling time that Arlyne and most caregivers were dreading. She was aware that William had, in the past, drawn maps of where he was going and how to get there before he ever left the house. Quite clever, but it didn't help how to get out of the parking lot. Arlyne never gave any ultimatum about not driving, but William made it rather simple, actually.

Arlyne recognized that each succeeding day was bringing increased requirements of more clearly supervised activities.

1999

William was not truly convinced it was time for himself to stop driving when he arrived home, and driving in the driveway, he said, "Do you know where the hell you are?"

As a result of today's support group meeting, he wrote a letter to CEO Annette Kelly at the Alzheimer's Association and asked if she had any information on Alzheimer's drivers. She answered quickly with several published items regarding this subject. That was the end of the concern. To wit, he wrote:

Dear Arlyne,

Please see article attached,
Alzheimer's Association National Newsletter: "Safety of Alzheimer's Drivers"
Use this note as proof of my commitment, and intention. I authorize (and deputize) you to tell me (early on) when you would prefer to drive, rather than WOG doing the driving. I promise not to disagree (keep this note as a record of my intentions).

This is preferable to an auto accident.

> Much love,
> Your husband
> William

A side note was added from him in the margin of the article:

AOG

> You tell me when I should no longer drive. I might even feel that way before you do.

> WOG

It was never a problem. He would occasionally test by saying, "I'll drive today."

At which time, Arlyne would politely and calmly say, "That's okay, I'll drive."

He was the eternal administrator. His profession was a hospital administrator, so he would often write Arlyne notes on a regular basis, only a few rooms apart, to present his momentary thinking.

NOTE TO ARLYNE:

> Arlyne agrees to schedule an appointment with Dr. Dreher to identify the reasons for my rapid deterioration of my memory.
> Today we visited Dr. Candor, a cardiologist, who feels that my atrial fibrillation, not my heart-status, is a contributor to my increasing problems.
> The potential for continued mini-strokes, unknown to me, caused by multi-infarct activity, could be erasing memory in small increments. Perhaps there is treatment which has minimal

downside, but offers some protection against these strokes (infarcts).

How about Coumadin (isn't this a more effective medicine than aspirin which I am presently taking?) Other medicines? Other alternatives?

Dr. Malinde says no! How about a visit to Dr. Dreher?

Your loving (persistent) husband,
What's his name?

William might have some memory problems, but he still retained his sense of humor. A standing ovation for that. An appointment was made with the neurologist Dr. Dreher.

February 9, 1999

Spells continued off and on all day.

March 2, 1999

William had dermatological basal cell carcinoma surgery on the right temple that required several stitches that involved two rather large areas. Staff had requested Arlyne's presence for clarification of their directions.

July 6, 1999

Now it was Arlyne's time for attention. She was going to have a back operation. William thought it was he who was going to have the operation. He asked what was the operation for and shouldn't a doctor know about this.

September 6, 1999

Labor Day was a nice family dinner of togetherness at a local restaurant. On their way home, William asked where Greg was tonight. Greg, his son-in-law, had been leading most of the conversations to compensate for William's disassociation. When they arrived home, Arlyne also found the sugar bowl in the refrigerator.

November 20, 1999

William entered Osceola Regional Hospital at 6:00 a.m. with heart in fibrillation. This was the second day that verapamil didn't work. He was admitted to the hospital, and Arlyne returned home about 7:00 p.m. At 10:15 p.m., there was a telephone call from the nurse, saying William wanted to talk to his wife. He was very confused and wanted to come home. He asked Arlyne where he was, and she tried to explain that he must remain in the hospital for a stress test in the morning. The nurse came on the phone and strongly suggested that it would be better if she would return to the hospital. They would prepare a chairbed for her next to William's bed.

When Arlyne arrived at hospital, William was completely dressed, had his heart monitor tucked in around his T-shirt, and had his shoes and socks in place also. Arlyne got him undressed and in bed at 11:30 p.m., all the while explaining the situation over and over.

"Are we in Newark? Are we driving or flying?" He heard a noise in the hall and got out of bed to find out the reason for the noise. He thought at the moment he was at home. All night long produced an endless diatribe of "Why are we here? Where am I? Are we here because of you or me?" He would stare around the room and request that they walked to their home. The questions continued. "What hospital is this? Are we at home in our bedroom?" Ad infinitum.

Arlyne finally got him to try sleeping, and he did but only in spurts. No sleep for Arlyne, however.

May 2000

At the Oyster Catcher Restaurant in Tampa, they met their friends, Edna and Frank, who lived quite close on Anna Maria Island, for brunch. Frank and William had remained close since being at the academy together many years ago. Driving back home, William wanted to know whom they met today and commented further that they seemed like a nice couple, and were they married?

Oy vey!

June 2000

The movie *The Passion* had arrived at the local theater, and Arlyne thought William might like to see it. She asked him, having explained it to him. He replied that he thought that would be good. They arrived at the theater and took their seats, and the movie began. It was probably the first few minutes of the movie, which was quite dark and the music was immediately somber, when he said, "I'll go out in the lobby and wait for you."

Of course, Arlyne followed him, and that was the end of that sojourn. Another lesson learned.

August 2000

William was invited to participate in a research project at University of Central Florida (UCF) by Dr. Janet Whiteside, executive director at the Center for Communication Disorders. He would attend UCF once a week for a sixteen-week program concerning Alzheimer's disease. Three other persons with Alzheimer's would be present, including the spouses. Each couple would have an associate master's intern accompanying them.

Each session began at a table for everyone playing various game requirements, which developed into fun time (e.g., What do you remember especially about 1941?). After the session, each couple moved to private sessions with the intern.

Various exercises were required to be performed at home, with time requirements and scores provided by the spouse. Each day, the exercises would continue for an hour, and if it became too arduous, the games would resume later.

Results were kept and always submitted to UCF. At the end and at the beginning of the research, testing was scheduled. A copy of the sixteen-week results was given to the participants. The results were detailed and impressive. It was all a wonderful and interesting experience with all the material that was expected to be completed and required of these individuals with Alzheimer's disease.

The associate master's intern assigned to William was very good and kind. Her son, age nineteen, was attending college in Gainesville and had recently broken his back from a fall. William and Arlyne would always ask about his recuperation. One day, when William asked about her son, she informed him that her son had died. No reason was given and was never asked.

The couple across the table from William and Arlyne was participating because the husband had Alzheimer's and had recently become a stutterer. His young son had committed suicide, and it was felt perhaps that was the reason for the stuttering.

They all enjoyed each other. William, of course, provided incidental comedic relief. Arlyne wondered later if he was selected for that, perhaps, necessary qualification and for that particular group. They had fun exchanges at the table. Jim, the third person at the table, would always remind everyone that he was planning a trip very soon with his RV. Incredibly, it was learned about two weeks after completing the research that Jim had been diagnosed with Parkinson's disease. Overwhelmed, he went out into his backyard and shot himself. An experience not shared with William. It was certainly an addition to a seemingly chain of inordinate happenings. A decidedly indelible memory for Arlyne.

August 31, 2000

An interesting interlude to the usual requirements and daily activities was very unexpectedly introduced. An invitation was extended to William and Arlyne to participate as part of a television series regarding persons with Alzheimer's. Sponsored by the Alzheimer's Association, Florida Department of Elder Affairs, the Christian Service Center, and Administration on Aging was a "Video Training Project for Homebound Caregivers" being filmed at Disney Institute Studios. Highlighting "Conversations with Those Who Care" were segments dealing with important challenges facing caregivers and issues surrounding facing diagnosis and immediately afterward. A great deal of helpful information was presented. *Ask the Doc* was another television program; Arlyne and William were invited to be panel members regarding Alzheimer's disease and the relationship and concerns facing caregivers and nutrition.

An interesting television program was presented on PBS channel regarding Alzheimer's disease as well. It was suggested to engage the person with Alzheimer's to watch and involve them in conversation concerning information that was presented.

William took issue with the "lost feeling that inside was a feeling of crisis in his life" and "memories define who you are." He acknowledged that memories are wonderful. "But they sure don't make who I am."

Regarding the statement that he had lost himself, he vehemently reacted with "Well, I certainly have not lost myself. I know I don't remember things, and I forget a lot, but I'm still my own person."

"A crisis in my life? I've never felt I had a crisis. I've never looked at problems as such, and I don't regard Alzheimer's as a 'crisis' because I have you. It's what you feel inside."

Gott sei Dank!

2001

USMMA appointed a new superintendent, Admiral Joseph Stewart. He was introduced to officers and staff at the Christmas Party in the Melville Hall, Officers Club, USMMA. The admiral had been a general in the US Marine Corps.

William, shaking hands with the admiral to welcome him and congratulate him, remarked, "This is the first time I have ever met a general admiral."

Admiral Stewart greatly appreciated the humor. Admiral Stewart became a big favorite at the academy.

March 26, 2001

It was mid-morning, and William complained of a sharp pain in the right-side back of his head and front shoulder. This lasted approximately twenty minutes and said he also felt this pain during early morning hours. He swallowed his meds and gradually felt better.

Heart medicine summary was in order since he had two previous cardiac catheterizations: quinidine, Quinaglute, Ecotrin, procainamide, Inderal, Lanoxin, digoxin, atenolol, and Tambocor (flecainide).

Alzheimer's meds available at this time: tacrine, Exelon, Reminyl, and Aricept (donepezil). Aricept was the doctor's choice for William.

October 6, 2001

Having learned that Kings Point Academy was the only one of the five federal military academies that had no honor society, alarm bells went off for William, and he felt that this omission should not exist for the midshipmen. This would supply the definite need to promote additional academic excellence. Consequently, it took some time, but the effort was led by Dr. Jane Brickman, head of the Humanities Department. Then eventually blessed and passed by the Maritime Administration (MARAD), Washington, DC: Admiral Stewart, superintendent; Sashi Kumar, dean of instruction; Captain Jim Tobin, president and CEO, Kings Point Alumni Foundation; and Dr. Arlyne O'Gara. This organization would also provide postgraduate scholarship opportunities as well as introduction to ongoing cultural events. The O'Gara Academic Honor Society (OAHS). Big hurrah for education!

November 10, 2001

At home, suddenly, William was feeling dizzy and had trouble walking, was generally unbalanced, and wanted to lie down. He said his body "felt funny" but had no pain. He went to bed, stayed there, and slept.

During the night, Arlyne detected William's respiration was fast and then became almost inaudible. This continued for over an hour. He didn't go walking the next morning, didn't get up, and stayed in bed all day except to eat lunch and dinner. He spoke as if in a daze, and it seemed difficult for him.

November 19, 2001

Insisting on calling Mel, a Kindergartener, about the West Side High School reunion in Cranford, New Jersey, he struck out after trying several phone calls. They finally connected and conversed for a long time. Arlyne then talked to Mel and then to his wife, Reggie. Later, William complained that Reggie wouldn't let him talk to Mel, so he wanted to call Mel later. No explanation would suffice, and he kept repeating that Reggie wouldn't let him talk to Mel. Arlyne seemed to be successful with "Let's call another time."

December 15, 2001

After a few weeks, he said, "Mel doesn't think I should go to the reunion." He hadn't talked to Mel at all. He told Frank, a classmate of high school days, that Arlyne didn't think he should go to the reunion. Arlyne overheard this conversation and corrected him.

"Oh, I guess I misunderstood. I haven't seen Mel in a long time. Maybe it won't be long before the reunion, right?"

Arlyne's explanatory mantra of many times over the weeks: "No plans for the reunion. Mel will surely let us know over the weeks." "No plans yet for any reunion. Mel will surely let us know, and we will go."

December 16, 2001

He woke this morning complaining of severe hurt in his left lower rib cage, saying, "Really bad. What could it be?"

Arlyne saw no bruises or redness and suggested it could be a pulled muscle from sneezing or coughing. He accepted that, but it didn't preclude the continuation of the same conversation twelve to fifteen times during the day.

December 18, 2001

William wanted to be helpful, turning on and off the inside and outside Christmas lights. The lights had already been disconnected at the socket level. A saving grace. Actually, Arlyne was weighing this small problem as being far less bothersome than having him always locking her out of the house. Recognizing the need to carry a key at all times solved that problem.

January 12, 2002

Dermatology revealed a melanoma on William's back. The surgeon requested Arlyne to be present during this fairly large surgery. *Questioning William's behavior was rather astute for an experienced staff,* she thought. A large surgery site, but everything was quite successful. Nevertheless, Arlyne had a questionable reaction to witnessing the cutting and removing at the surgery site.

February 12, 2002

Dr. Dreher had suggested an examination and blood test by Dr. Holmes, a hematologist. While in Dr. Holmes's waiting room, William looked at Arlyne and remarked while staring in her face, "Are you as beautiful as I think you are?"

The big lump in her throat just wouldn't go away.

William was examined, blood was drawn, x-rays were done, and a few other incidental tests were done. An appointment was made for the results.

February 18, 2002

Six days later, William and Arlyne were requested to come to Dr. Holmes's office at their first opportunity. The next day, they visited Dr. Holmes and were escorted to a cozy small room with overstuffed, comfortable large chairs—an ambiance not found in a doctor's office. Was it, perchance, a sixth sense kicking in that sent this chill up her spine and a knot in the pit of her stomach, as Arlyne, with clenched teeth, entered the room to the unknown.

Dr. Holmes, with obvious consideration and gentility, reviewed the results of William's examination. They found some areas of moderate problems: cholesterol, urine, heart palpitations, and some lesser items not problematic. However, they did find, after detailed scrutinizing of all possibilities, that there were cancer cells present in the blood; in fact, two separate cancers of the blood: polycythemia, cancer of the red blood cells, and thrombocytosis, cancer in the platelets.

The next question was, What could be done about it? The doctor offered the availability of a medicine, but the other approach they found more patient-friendly was to come to the clinic once a month to have blood drawn. This would be about an hour and a half investment of time. That was agreeable to William, and he accepted it all quite well. Arlyne wondered if he realized the extent of these results.

He did become aware later, however, of the severity, perhaps when he vociferously objected to his blood being tossed into a trash can. A routine that was altered the following month with the relocation of the trash can. The nurse did explain to him that this was diseased blood, not allowed to be reused. He listened politely but didn't seem to be at all convinced.

March 15, 2002

A summarized list of medical maladies that required ongoing care and assessment: polycythemia, thrombocytosis, atrial fibrillation, chronic obstructive pulmonary disease (COPD), melanoma, hypothyroidism, Alzheimer's disease, lupus erythematosus, and dermatological continuation.

Blood cancer diagnoses were almost the straw for Arlyne, but she knew only too well that tears helped nothing and that she had to be stronger than ever. This was a reminder of the malevolence of diseases on various levels and to reassess her situation within this realm. She had always been William's sounding board, his assistant, his right hand, his "emory" board, his alter ego, and his health protector, warts and all. In other words, William was the love of her life—actually, her life on which he was dependent. No way could she deny that.

William was now seventy-four years old. Compassion, patience, and always respect—Arlyne gave all in loving doses. She never treated him like a child, would encourage his making decisions, gave him choices as many times as possible, and never, never argued with him or his choices. These were lessons learned early on.

The all-time valuable and rewarding lesson for Arlyne was believing in the benefit of the tactile opportunities and the results. Hugging, patting his hand, sometimes just holding his hand, kissing his forehead, and telling him she loved him all helped to make a great difference in his behavior. She felt strongly that all these activities reinforced the feeling of security and, for a person with Alzheimer's, the feeling of security, which was high on their list of needs. William tried so hard to do what Arlyne asked of him. He really wanted to please her. No show of tantrums, nor meanness, nor resorting to bad language. How tremendously blessed she felt. It had been said that the caregiver woke up to the same tourist, wanting to take exactly the same tour. Maybe that was a blessing, too, Arlyne opined.

During their married and active life, William and Arlyne planned for the two of them to do everything together. He never took sole credit for anything. It was always "and my wife." With all the increasing possible hair-pulling situations, how could she possibly get upset with someone who told her, almost daily, how important she was to him and how fortunate he was to have her love and to have her to love.

There was never a question of giving her entire attention and love to this wonderful person.

Vive la Alzheimer's!

Of the three stages of Alzheimer's—early, middle, and late—William was now entering the middle to late stage, as far as Arlyne could understand stages. He still shaved himself and fed himself but needed help with the nail-trimming and a mélange of other daily necessaries. She had also realized the increasing need for support in almost everything else he did.

July 18, 2002

At home, making a special trip from his office to Arlyne's office, a matter of forty feet inside the house, he pulled himself up to his full six feet and, with unquestioned authority, said to her, "Isn't it about time you planned a trip for us?"

This was a bit of a shock because, first and foremost, she never did the planning. He did. Ignoring that fact, she replied, "I guess so!"

Now what, and how does she handle this one?

September 19, 2002

After a few agonizing days of weighing alternatives, Arlyne decided a short cruise might serve the purpose. She knew it would delight him. They could drive to Port Canaveral easily, and on a Caribbean cruise, he would not only be safely corralled but have crowds of people with whom to interact.

It was a short, five-day Caribbean cruise. William was really elated but didn't have a clue about preparing, although that was expected. He enjoyed it greatly, with unbelievable balance, and his jovial mien and sense of humor all came forth. Arlyne was so pleased it was working wonderfully well. When William got up in the middle of the night, Arlyne always tried to keep one eye opened until he returned to bed in case he had any kind of problem. One particular night, he arose to go to the bathroom about 2:00 a.m. Arlyne thought he had been in there much too long and felt she should check if he was all right. She knocked at the bathroom door and called, "Are you okay?"

There was no response. When he didn't respond after a few attempts, she opened the door, and the bathroom was empty. Panicsville! Now what to do? The first thought was, of course, he went overboard. When sanity returned, Arlyne knew he wouldn't be able to open the patio door because it was much too heavy. She looked out in the passageway and nary a soul was stirring at 2:00 a.m., so she called the purser and outlined her predicament that he was missing completely and gave his name, age, and cabin number. To describe him, she had to admit he was wearing his pajamas, socks, and a watch hat. Not an alluring picture, but an unusual picture, to be sure.

The moments were months, but Arlyne finally received a call from the purser saying they had probably found William, and he was fine and safely engaged in conversation with a lovely young lady working at the desk two decks below. He was able to use the elevator by himself. Yo! Arlyne hurriedly made her way to retrieve him. Hug him or strangle him? Of course, she smiled and asked, "Did you have a good time?"

To which he replied, "I don't remember, but I know I must have had a great time!"

Arlyne made an immediate, firm decision that this was definitely their last trip (2002).

2003

They attended church service, which was a surprise that William opted to go. They were sitting in the pew, and when it was time to kneel, he did and then zeroed in on the lone little gray-haired lady kneeling in front of them. He reached out and gently tapped her on the shoulder. She turned and smiled at William; at which time, he said, "How does your hair look today?"

At first, she had a doubtful expression and immediately looked at Arlyne, who just smiled and shook her head. Last time to church.

September 2, 2003

Having arrived at their daughter's home, greeted by all four in the family, they were all looking forward to a special dinner. A half hour after arriving, William surreptitiously came to Arlyne and asked if she was ready to go home. He had been lost four times in the house. They returned to their own home before having dinner. Always be prepared.

October 14, 2003

William's roommate, Bobby Jo, from USMMA, some fifty-three years ago, had kept in touch over the years. He and his wife had visited numerous times. With preplanning, Bobby Jo had arrived three days before by train from San Diego and planned to stay a week. William asked Arlyne, "Who is that man in there?"

She explained. Later in the evening, while all three were conversing in the living room, William turned to Bobby Jo and said, "Just who are you?"

He answered, "Bobby Jo."

To which William answered, "No, you aren't. I don't know who you are."

That was a tearjerker. A guestimate would have said that William had lost about the last thirty-five years or more.

October 16, 2003

A wonderfully positive remark today from William to Arlyne: "You know you make me feel secure with you."

Arlyne thought, *Who could ask for more? Thank you, Lord.*

William continued to do physically well, comparatively, on the current daily meds. Although he had not taken his daily two-mile walks in over a year, he still told everyone that he walked every day.

Other problems had also come upon the scene, such as incontinence and help with bathing and dressing. Arlyne had learned to barber him over the years too.

October 20, 2003

Arlyne decided to enumerate some of the many facets she had learned and had put into practice during her days of William's Alzheimer's. It was helpful to remind herself on an interim basis. The requirements seemed to be increasing daily, sometimes by leaps and bounds. Her list was varied but always with underlying concern and the values of love and respect.

- Keep simplifying the house by clearing clutter as much as possible. Put breakables and valuables out of the way.
- Remember that items outside can be particularly danger-ous, such as ladders, the pool, or even garage shelves.
- Keep consistency inside the house by not changing much and only as they are needed.
- Keep familiar things around (albums, cards, pictures, and memorabilia).
- Replace night lights always as needed, especially for night-time trips to the bathroom.
- Remember the need for handrails at commode, tub or shower, and outside steps.
- Have serious discussions about problems that could arise down the road.
- Remember to remove medicines from easy access.
- Keep searching for paths to help and therapy.
- Avoid possible threat of scalding water and must be checked out occasionally by lowering temperature on the water heater.
- Place electric appliances on kitchen countertop, out of sight.

Arlyne kept adding to this list as time elapsed, and she felt she benefited from timely reviewing and constantly adding to it.

Additional personal responsibilities they once shared were now completely the onus for Arlyne. Planning for future concerns, such as healthcare, legal, and finances must be faced. Her business experience background had, to a degree, prepared her for most of these profound and complex requirements.

Coping skills continued to be demanding, for no one can anticipate where or when in the brain those plaques of amyloids and tangles would decide to misbehave. Arlyne had really tried to approach many of the problems in their entirety—so many facets. Thankfully and gratefully, she found this approach also resulted in finding more love inside than she ever knew she had. A card on Arlyne's desk read "It's not a burden but an opportunity." A positive evaluation was necessary to survive in most evaluations, she had decided. Necessary, too, to have consideration for her own health. Arlyne resolved to make a few personal appointments. Yes!

November 15, 2003

Folding four pairs of pants from the dryer, William said to Arlyne, "Why don't you have someone that's here do that for you?"

Who else was there?

He was smiling about, completely brushing his teeth, and Arlyne said, "You seem to be happy about it!"

He replied, "I'm happy about everything."

And thankfully, he was.

He appeared in the kitchen. "Can you come with me? It will only take thirty seconds."

He led her to the bedroom and, standing at the foot of the bed, pointed to Arlyne's side of the bed and said, "Do you see it? You are right there with only your nose showing."

Now that was a puzzle to explain. How could he think she could be standing right beside him and be in bed? Houdini she was not.

December 2003

Arlyne became quite ill for several days with bronchitis, coughing continually, not eating, and not sleeping. Antibiotics and cough syrup did help. She was entirely exhausted from the situation, and William said, "Don't you feel okay?"

She replied, "No," and tried to explain, taking all her strength, that she was sick, s-i-c-k.

He looked at her and said, "Now what did you have planned for us to do this afternoon and tonight?"

How do you commit hari-kari? She needed a "hankerfish!"

William came to the kitchen while Arlyne was cleaning up dinner work and asked, "Where is the fish?"

"Fish, what fish?"

"The fish for the people."

"I don't know."

"Oh, forget it."

"Okay."

He had on trousers that he wore to the restaurant. "Do I wear these to bed?"

February 2, 2004

On TV, movies were not a choice anymore. He wanted only up things, nothing sad or down things. It was mostly basketball games and only if Arlyne watched with him. What were the scores? What did that mean? Who was that player? Hardly any understanding at all.

Watching a basketball game on TV, William was in his white terry cloth robe and was desperately trying to get his pant belt over the robe. He worked and worked at it until he finally got his pant belt buckled. Arlyne asked him what he was trying to do; to which he replied he was trying to get his seat belt on. "Did you get yours on? Oh, I thought we were on a plane."

"I think about this once in a great while, but I thought about Herman [Kindergartener]. What did he die from?"

This was asked over and over, during morning coffee, every time they went in the car, and usually each evening while they watched TV.

Having lunch with Doyle, a dear friend, Doyle asked William if he still went walking. "Oh yes! Every day!"

It had been one and a half years that he hadn't walked.

March 12, 2004

On the way to get groceries, Arlyne thought she would take William by TCBY, a little out of the way, but he loved the frozen yogurt there. He said, "Okay."

They arrived, parked, walked to the store, and entered. He said, "I don't want any."

A good scream was in order.

William was worried about someone looking in the front windows at home, although they had been etched for twenty years. "What can we do to cover these windows so people can't see in?"

A message he wrote on scrap paper to Arlyne: "AOG close Venetian CORP [to keep] people outside, from people posside, from OUTSIDE looking look in! WOG."

Arlyne felt she had missed the course in encryption.

March 24, 2004

"Where are we going tonight?"

They had been invited to Hollis's graduation at 7:00 p.m., University of Central Florida. She was receiving her master's degree.

"Why are we going? Can't you go without me?"

They arrived there, and he seemed to enjoy the trip. After ten minutes, they had met a few people who had started to arrive, and William said, "I want to go home."

He kept this up until they had to leave.

During the return trip home, he asked, "Is this our car or a rental? What hotel are we staying at? In Florida?" Arlyne thought, *Anyone have a sedative?*

William woke Arlyne in the middle of the night, shook her shoulder, and just smiled at her.

She asked, "Are you okay?"

He mumbled and went back to sleep.

He had also been waking her every morning by shaking her or pulling her pillow from under her head for no understandable reason.

April 15, 2004

William was getting lost in the house, not knowing which way to go to the bedroom or any other room. He did not like Arlyne reading the paper. One of his newly obvious problems was aphasia.

May 8, 2004

William enjoyed eating out on the patio. The table was set when he came out.

"Oh! Did they send this over?"

"Who are 'they'?"

"The hotel."

"We are at home."

"We are?"

"How many nights are we staying here?"

June 22, 2004

They were watching the sunset at early evening from the patio and extolling the beauty of the lake and the surroundings. William asked, "Where does the sun come from?"

"Let's get up early tomorrow and watch it come up" was the final attempt after trying a simplified explanation.

October and November became "Octemblar" and "Novie." Hair became the dominating topic in most conversations. William could not pronounce *horizon* or *Passaic*. Of course, the persistent questions continued: "Is this our apartment?" "Do we have another someplace?" "Is there a man staying in here [bedroom]?"

After watching forty-five minutes of a TV football game that William had selected, he asked, "What are we watching?"

July 28, 2004

Robert and Hagen, his neighbors, brought some cupcakes to the house. William found Arlyne in her office and told her that the men from the university were there, but they would be back. Robert and Hagen were in the kitchen.

August 9, 2004

The Hurricane Charlie hit the area at 8:30 p.m. on August 9, 2004, with 150 mile-per-hour winds. William was already in bed and had to be wakened in order to seek safety in the interior walk-in closet. Arlyne explained several times and wondered if she did get him to lie down on the floor mattress, how would she ever get him back up? He finally agreed and was able to lie down.

It was a rocky night, wondering if they would have a house in the morning. William, however, slept through the storm. Arlyne thanked God. Daylight came, and they opened the front door to the destruction of all forms of landscaping, with seven felled trees. They couldn't even find the driveway and pool enclosure, and the roofs were both gone. The inconveniences mounted, and the difficult requirements and acquisitions for necessary repairs continued for at least six months. Charlie was very unwelcome. After almost three months, they were happily and finally getting a new roof. William was most upset with all the noise and constant hammering. Explanations of getting a new roof were needed every five minutes. He was constantly looking for Arlyne and, when he found her, would say that there was someone in the house or there was someone who wanted to get in.

September 3, 2004

William was going to bed earlier and earlier (7:30 p.m.). His speech had also become quite difficult to understand, and he rambled on about things no one knew about. He placed two large pots of artificial flowers in front of the inside front door one evening. When he was inside the garage and went up the steps to the inside, he paused and asked, "Now where do I go?"

September 13, 2004

It concerned Arlyne that William seldom seemed to be at home but always traveling or in a hotel. Perhaps that shouldn't be so strange, reviewing his past years of constant traveling.

September 15, 2004

A lovely vacation was planned to be with their family at Cape Hatteras, Outer Banks. It was a lovely home, and they had long walks around the block, put jigsaw puzzles together, and waded in the pool. William never did figure out that they weren't at home nor at a hotel. He kept wanting to call for a wake-up call, for a coffee, or to order from the menu.

Returning home by car was a nightmare. How long to the airport or to the hotel? And then he was on a ship or on a train. The conductor wouldn't get him a berth because he was tired and wanted to lie down. Then it became the whys: Why aren't we going to a hotel? Arlyne talked William into laying his head on her lap. He rested somewhat, but when he sat up again, he was stoic, as opposed to the previous nonstop talking. Arlyne was never happier to arrive home.

William had to have help for the order of dressing and undressing. What to take off first, next, etc. He watched what Arlyne ate, when and how, and went from there. His appetite was not what it should be, but he always had room for ice cream.

September 25, 2004

Walking around the house had definitely become a chore and caused complaints of back pain. He had two different MRIs that found a bulge in one vertebra plus thinning of the pads between the discs. Perhaps part of the aging process. On one occasion, Arlyne had to get a wheelchair to get William from the commissary to the car. After that, he sat at the commissary and waited for her to shop. Arlyne thought it was time to get a wheelchair.

September 26, 2004

William's speech was worsening. He had difficulty selecting and pronouncing words. His speech became monotonal, slurred, and hardly audible at times.

At 7:15 p.m., William wanted Arlyne to go through the house with him to see if the lights were on that she wanted. All kinds of lights were on: dining room chandelier, other lamps in the living room, etc. She usually had only night lights on throughout the house. Give points for thoughtfulness?

He put pants on backward and didn't know it. It seemed not possible that he didn't know it, but the current problem needed to have current help, she resolved.

October 4, 2004

William asked what his rank in the military was because he forgot. Arlyne asked why he wanted to know, and he said because he wanted to be sure to say the right things when the military came that evening because "You know I can't talk."

After going to bed, he advised her to let the police in for the business. When asked what business, he replied, "The lunch and things like that. You know I can't tell."

William wanted to go to the mailbox for mail. "Where does he drop it?" In the mailbox. "Where is that?" In thirty-five years, it hasn't moved.

November 2, 2004

Breakfast bread with morning coffee. It was buttered and put on a tray. He wanted to add jelly to it. The butter was pointed out to him. He was nonplussed about where to put the jelly. He asked if he should put it on the underside of the bread.

In the evening, Arlyne asked if William wanted ice cream. He said, "When did I ever say no?"

It was another strange, undecipherable explanation.

"Did you bake bookies [cookies]?"

Arlyne was sitting in an easy chair in the bedroom, and he said, "You are really beautiful, not just outside but inside too."

Wow! Could anyone be more fortunate. After forty-three years of togetherness too.

November 15, 2004

They were having dinner on the patio and looking along the lake edge. Actually, it was a lake drawdown, and there was no water but only sand out there.

"I see a ballerina down there." He was motioning out to the lake.

"Is she dancing?"

"No, she's en pointe."

"What color hair does she have?"

"Just yucky, not brown, not blond. Are the people having pasta?"

"Who?"

"The people over there and the ones here." He was pointing to opposing sides.

Who needed television?

William didn't want Arlyne to read. He wanted all her attention. While cleaning the bedroom around him, he asked, "Just five minutes, but how long are we staying here? What time is it? What day is this?"

December 2, 2004

Around midnight, William rapped on Arlyne's shoulder. She had been asleep.

"Are you okay? Everything all right?"

"Did you have enough sleep? Did you oversleep?"

"No, it's midnight." He ignored that.

"Are you all packed? Where is Leneita [Arlyne's sister]? Is she with us?"

"No, she's not here. No, she's not coming."

"She should come with us."

About 2:00 a.m., William was up and wandering in the other end of the house and back to the bedroom, then back to the other end of the house. Arlyne went looking for him and met him in the laundry room.

"What are you doing?"

"I'm looking for Arlyne. I want to tell her where I am so she doesn't think I've been in an accident or something."

"Well, come with me, and we'll get this solved."

They went to the bedroom, and Arlyne persuaded him to get in bed. She tucked him in, promising she would call Arlyne and tell her, okay? Arlyne got back in bed again. After about two minutes of quiet, the conversation resumed.

"I think it would be better if I called Arlyne and talked to her."

"I talked to her and explained where you are, and she was fine with that."

"Maybe I better call her. What did she say?"

"It's all okay and that she would talk to you when it got light outside and glad you are getting some rest."

William awoke at 6:00 a.m., turned all the lights on, and walked around. Arlyne coaxed him back to bed, saying that she'd like to get some more rest. This scenario sent Arlyne into a bit of a depression when she reviewed all of it. It was all so incredibly sad. Over coffee, total confusion continued as to where he was. "How come the cat was here? Did we bring him along? Was that our blanket?"

December 10, 2004

When Arlyne tried to make conversation, she quickly lost him. William just seemed so far away and would begin to look at a paper as though she was not there. Yet most of the time, if she were so much as a closet away, he called for her.

Returning from the commissary in the car there was the continuation of questions.

"Where are we going now?"

"Home."

"Where is home?"

"Kissimmee."

"Now, is that in Florida?"

"Yes."

"How long will we stay there?"

"Will we be meeting the Kindergartener guys for dinner? Mel?"

"No, he is in New Jersey. We are in Florida."

"Is this our car?"

They were nearing King's Highway, a road very near the house.

"Do you know where you are?"

"Definitely. Grandview Boulevard."

"Is this the right street? How long will we stay here? Is this the right driveway?"

December 18, 2004

Watching basketball players on TV, William remarked that their heads were all "raized." He meant shaved with a razor. He asked Arlyne what she thought about walking, and she said she thought it was a good thing to do. He agreed, saying that it made him feel good each day to do that and it didn't hurt him at all. He hadn't walked in over two years.

December 21, 2004

William answered a telephone call and wrote it down: "CALLED BY I know last but. I can't find fast name? name?"

They played twenty questions a lot. Arlyne couldn't understand what he was talking about so many times, and she tried so hard. It ended in frustration for both.

The support group meeting was in the Miller Building, and they had attended for eight years. Sometimes, on the way, William questioned where they were going, and it was always "to the support group."

They would arrive and go inside. He no longer recognized the entrance to the building or in what room the meeting was held. The remembering "hole" was getting smaller and smaller, and the misunderstanding of meaningful questions and situations kept Arlyne at the ready.

January 6, 2005

Referring to Doyle, his only partner in Prison Health for fifteen years, William said, "Who is Doyle? Where does he fit in?"

At home, in bed, he asked, "How long are we staying here? Did someone give this to us? How did we get this place?"

An exterminator was busy upstairs in the garage to resolve an invading squirrel issue, and Arlyne explained the problem. He asked, "Why are you doing that? You shouldn't have to do that in an apartment."

William wanted to set the alarm clock and finally gave up. "You better do this." He could not tell time on a nondigital clock.

He asked three different times when they were going to the funeral for the little girl. No little girl, and no funeral.

He wanted to go to Macaroni's Restaurant for dinner, a pick from a choice of three. They drove through a downpour, and Arlyne drove William up to the entrance. Arlyne sloshed through the rain after parking the car, they sat down in the restaurant, and he said he wanted to go home for dinner. So they went home, and Arlyne prepared dinner. What was the alternative?

January 8, 2005

"What's that picture doing on the wall?"

Arlyne explained it was her high school picture at graduation. William said he knew that, but what was it doing on that wall? She explained that it was his bedroom wall. Rather a bit chagrined, he quietly related that he thought he was someplace else.

With no conversation, he would occasionally utter an "uh-huh" into the silence, as if he was talking to himself, "yup."

Out of nowhere, he would say, "I really have fun when we are together. You are fun to be with."

Arlyne replied, "It's because I love you."

Then he would say, "You make me feel secure." Manna from heaven!

William carefully related all the steps it took him to remove, by ladder, the overgrown philodendron from the tree in the front yard. It was preventing the spotlight on the tree to light the house at night as it should. After retrieving the ladder, he said, "I just put it up against the tree, carefully cut the leaves, and now the light shines through to the house."

Wonderful, although he had never done any of that at all. Arlyne had done that several days before using a long pole with a saw at the end of it.

January 15, 2005

Arlyne noticed a drop of bloody urine on the bathroom floor. William complained of being dizzy, and she quickly undressed him and got him to bed. He seemed all right after that, but he was cold and had great difficulty telling her he needed another blanket.

William's tremors had also increased. Holding a dish or glass became impossible at times. Walking and balance were much worse. He didn't want to go anyplace. He kept saying, "I'm tired and I want to stay in bed."

The wheelchair was not much help. Only seldom did William agree to being pushed down the road for an outing.

February 12, 2005

The support group had become minimally enjoyable for William. Arlyne thought it would probably be best to stay at home.

The O'Gara Library of the Alzheimer's Association had become an informative boon to many caregivers and professionals since it opened in 2000.

Since 2002, Annette Kelly, MSN, ARNP, and CEO of the Alzheimer's Association, Central and North Florida Chapter, had initiated a marvelously original offering called "The O'Gara Library Lecture Series." Peggy Bargmann was a most talented leader in these events as well.

Enormously successful, these free lectures were scheduled monthly for persons with Alzheimer's disease or a related dementia, family caregivers, healthcare professionals, students, and anyone interested in learning more and meeting other people who found these lectures informative and empowering.

These lectures featured panels consisting of professionals in a specific field, caregivers, and others knowledgeable in the topic. The subjects covered were so useful and appropriate, generating great public interest from 2002 through 2005.

Just a few of the lecture titles indicated their usefulness:

- Resources, Research, and Technology
- Recognizing the Spiritual Dimension in Alzheimer's Disease
- Safety in the Home
- Finding Your Answers
- Ethical Issues in Alzheimer's Care
- Treating the Behavioral Symptoms of Dementia with Medication
- Communication Strategies for Persons with Memory Impairment
- Understanding and Living with Alzheimer's Disease

February 23, 2005

William attended some of these lectures but, at this point, probably didn't recognize that his giving, kind heart was at the core of these offerings. He always wanted to enhance any prospect of education, recognizing that "Knowledge is power" (Sir Francis Bacon). Arlyne had always privately lamented the fact that of all the existing maladies in this world, Alzheimer's disease, a brain disease, would be the attacker of William's God-given and outstanding mental abilities. Ours not to reason why.

March 3, 2005

About 8:00 p.m., returning from Orlando after having attended the O'Gara Library Lecture Series, William asked Arlyne:

"Do you have anyone at home?"

"Do you mean, is there anyone there besides me when we get home?" she questioned.

"Yes," he quickly replied.

"No, there's no one at home. Who do you think might be there?"

"I don't know."

"Who am I?" she quizzed.

"I'm not quite sure."

"Well, let's try to find out. You are?" she asked.

"I have a daughter, and she's married to Greg. Where are we?"

"Florida, Orlando, and we are on our way home, and we'll be there in about fifteen minutes." Another sticky wicket.

Dr. Cartwright, an ophthalmologist, gave William the results of earlier eye tests. He said that William had had a stroke but couldn't tell how long ago. Arlyne told the doctor that William had had no major stroke but TIAs, and the doctor offered the information that TIAs are prestroke events and that William had lost eyesight at the outer half of each eye (homonymous hemianopsia).

March 14, 2005

On the return trip home from having attended Respite, William talked every moment. Arlyne felt like a prisoner in the car and was about to go over the edge. He was looking at a magazine that said 2005, and he had figured out that it was the year 2000 and the fifth day.

It had become a useless attempt to try to get William to understand some everyday happenings. He wanted so much to be helpful at times, but just bringing the trash can from the road to the house had become a major chore.

William was most uncooperative at Respite, which was scheduled for four hours. After three days of Respite and not enjoying any of it, Arlyne couldn't expose him any longer to this unhappiness, and he didn't return again. When picking him up at Respite the last time, William said, "Do I have to go back there after we have lunch? Was I there last night? What did they find? Does Leneita know I have been in the hospital?"

He hadn't been in a hospital in many a moon.

"Do you know where you are?"

"Of course, I don't. Are we in Philly?"

"Did you have a good time?"

"I don't remember, but I know I must have had a great time though."

A happy camper.

March 16, 2005

Watching a basketball game in TV, in the middle of the game, William turned to Arlyne:

"Does my wife know where I am?"

"Oh yes! She knows."

"Okay." And that was the end of it.

William asked Arlyne if they were going to the West Side basketball game. West Side High School was where he had gone to high school in Newark, New Jersey.

Arlyne got William all shaved, showered, dressed, hair combed, and walked to the kitchen in preparation for getting in the car. She had a few minor things to clean up in the kitchen and asked him to sit down a minute. When he arose, he and the chair were all wet through and through. Somehow, he had got the pad she had placed in his shorts all crumpled up. Back to the bedroom, where a complete change of clothing was necessary.

Arlyne couldn't understand what William was trying to say.

"Did you ask how many years we have been together?"

He shook his head yes.

"Forty-four years."

He laughed.

"You're not my wife."

"Then who am I?"

"My mother."

"I am your mother?"

"Yes."

Time for a stiff upper lip.

March 18, 2005

Having dinner on trays on the patio, contained a glass of wine, chicken, and sweet potatoes. William took his fork, stabbed a piece of chicken, and dipped it in the glass of wine. Arlyne told him no, and William did it again. A note for the memory book that "no" did not work.

Arlyne put William in bed.

"Why are you doing this, Anna, Lana, Loanna?"

"Because I love you, and I want to make you comfortable."

"No!"

"What's my name?" She thought he said Lana.

"Okay, let's get you tucked in."

He mumbled something not understandable. Perhaps it was just as well to be left at that.

It was breakfast and the first time William refused to take his pills. He looked at them a million times, turning them over and over.

"Please take them. They are to keep you in good health."

He shook his head, and Arlyne took a final stance.

"Then that's okay. Do what you want." And left the room.

When Arlyne returned in about ten minutes, William was still looking at the pills but, finally, picked up his coffee cup and took the pills. She helped him up, he smiled, and she gave him a kiss.

"Now I guess you want a little nap."

"Yes."

Amen!

William was led to the bedroom to take a nap. He lay down on Arlyne's usual side of the bed, and later, she found him sitting in her usual lounge chair. That was a first.

March 29, 2005

So many happenings had become not only more numerous but also more difficult. Arlyne, at a low point herself, concluded that it was definitely time to reassess what had been done, what needed to be done for the future, and how to do it.

What had been done successfully was important for her own self-esteem, to recognize that her efforts had been done with love. Love does not conquer all, however, but at the end of a thirty-six-hour day and one collapses, love was certainly a comfort.

Retrospective learnings:

- Effectively keep records of illnesses, medications, and doctors.
- Know that all general information issued for all persons with Alzheimer's need not be applicable to William. William did not have aggressive behavior and did not have a history of being angry nor using unacceptable language.
- Constantly and willingly make necessary adjustments to his gradually increasing inabilities and addressing these changing needs with patience—this helped Arlyne personally as well.
- Find some personal time to unwind.

- Remain and retain a gentle, calm, and loving attitude.
- Remember that the tactile approach really worked. Holding William's hands when he seemed to be agitated, kissing on the forehead, telling him he was loved, gentle patting when passing by his chair, and repeating that together, they will face all odds.
- Remember that experience proved to Arlyne that the entire tactile approach produced and determined security, and security determined behavior.
- Take constant reassurance and agreement.
- Learn to change the subject when needed.
- Give simple answers.
- Look straight in his eyes and his face during conversations.
- Tell stories about when they met and other good times together.
- Know that it really mattered what you said and how you said it.
- Remember that to praise, a pat on the back was valuable to William.
- Remember that arguing had no merit at all. Agreeing and quickly changing the subject worked quite well, as did "therapeutic lying."
- Limit the necessity of making choices. Decision-making had become increasingly difficult, so eliminating the need for a choice meant having fewer choices available.
- Adapt to William's behavior as changes progressed in his responses.

So many little happenings emerged daily that Arlyne automatically met and resolved as possible problems or dangers.

It had been fourteen loving years of education to facilitate all these matters, and probably more, but Arlyne felt that experience did give rewards. Of course, being blessed to have a mostly cooperative person trying so hard to do what she asked meant many, many thanks to the Lord too.

As a high school principal, education, of course, was the priority. It also applied when a student misbehaved or appeared in Arlyne's office. The challenge remained, What did you learn from this difficult experience? "Never waste any opportunity to have learned a lesson for the future," Arlyne always reminded the student. Remembering her own advice, she strongly felt she needed to review what she had learned and transmit that into future positive terms.

Being aware of William's limited days ahead, Arlyne realized that she must become cognizant of the overwhelming and heart-rending and seemingly intolerable future needs. It seemed so sorrowful to even consider, but hard decisions must be made and given thorough planning. Arlyne wondered with all her being if she could do this. She told herself that she could and she must.

Arlyne began by investigating available assisted living accommodations in the area and making a list of needed information.

- Where are they located?
- What are the services offered? When are these available?
- What are the costs involved? What medical information and documents should be provided?
- How are doctor visits scheduled?
- What clothing is needed? Laundry?
- What is the routine for healthcare costs, doctor expenses, and any other expenses?
- What are the visiting guidelines?

If a nursing home was needed, she would answer these same previous questions.

The next step was to prepare funeral arrangements. Arlyne wisely decided to make these preparations as quickly as possible. The final days would become tremendously difficult and extremely emotional, so it would be quite helpful to have these arrangements at the ready. What would those needs be?

- Assemble all insurance papers, wills, death certificates, and billing statements (hospital and rehab center)

- Preplan funeral services—select funeral director, select interment or cremation, and select where or when
- Select a friend or responsible person who would be dependable to make notification contacts
- Have a list of people for notification, with telephone numbers or email addresses
- Preplan reception after funeral—where and when
- Prepare for this emotional separation with William and give him reassurance

On Arlyne's desk was a plaque that held these few words that she had learned to internalize and depend upon: "Not a burden but an opportunity." A time for profound convincing.

April 8, 2005

William asked, "Why do I have two rings on this finger?"
Arlyne asked, "How many watches do you have on your arm?"
"Two, maybe three."
Actually, he had one ring and one watch.

April 12, 2005

A disturbing event. William fell from the patio to the garden; two steps he probably didn't see. Thank God, he had only a scrape on his wrist.

April 13, 2005

William fell in the bathroom, and Arlyne arrived at the bathroom to see him pushing himself up, hair mussed, and face quite red. When asked how he fell, he didn't know.
"Were you dizzy?"
"I think so."

April 14, 2005

A plague of unbelievable hiccups began one day. After two days of trying practically everything on the computer and every old wives' tale, Arlyne called Dr. Stuart and took William to his office. William was given an injection to go into REM. It didn't work at all. He got a prescription filled for promethazine; four pills over sixteen hours. William stopped hiccupping after six days of immense, big-time stress. There was no way to prepare for such eventualities.

Arlyne became rather alarmed because William seemed so generally disabled. He wanted only to stay in bed. He could not speak at all and didn't see food or a glass of water in front of him. Arlyne had to give him a bed bath after a quickie haircut.

May 3, 2005

So as not to embarrass William, Arlyne typically gave Dr. Dreher, the neurologist, a written summary of William's general condition when they arrived for an appointment. She always outlined items such as personality, walking status, speech, eating status, incontinence, memory, and any new events, as follows:

Personality—continues to be the same, sweet, gentle, kind person with no obvious depression. Tries to read, but, of course, doesn't absorb anything. Difficulty following happenings or sequences of conversations. Modus operandi has changed; doesn't sleep as much during the day, increased wandering through the house. I can't be out of his sight for more than 15 minutes or he would come looking for me. Attended respite care only three days because he was not happy there. William gave the facilitator a hard time wondering where I was and when was I coming for him. A non-participant. He did not seem to be at home and much of the time didn't know where home was. "Are the bags packed in the car? How many days are we staying here?"

Walking—William scuffs as he walks, leans forward, falls forward at times, leans sideways and then must sit down

Speech—Very slurred, tonal change, invents new words when he can't find the proper word. Pronunciation very difficult especially when tired. I have to give up understanding.

Eating—Fairly stable. Eats much better at home. Edibles that require chewing are the most problematic.

Incontinence—Continually increasing (bladder only).

Memory—Centers around people and events of approximately 30 years ago. Does not recognize home area nor the environs, surprised when we arrive home in the driveway, can't figure out the sequence of dressing/undressing, brushing teeth, etc.

Events—Awakens at 3 A.M., wanders through the house, which he had never done before. Third time around, I caught up to him and asked what he was doing and he replied that he was looking for Arlyne to tell her where he was so she wouldn't worry, that he'd been in an accident. I encourage him back to the bedroom and into bed, all the while promising to get in touch with Arlyne. A second similar event. In the midst of trying to watch a TV basketball game, "Does my wife know where I am?" I assure him with great confidence and it all seems to pass.

Physical—William seems to be doing well with cardio problems, polycythemis, thrombocytosis and thyroid. All meds have remained the same.

No matter when they had visited Dr. Dreher, William had an enjoyable experience. Dr. Dreher was always so nonplussed with William's reaction to the Mini Mental State Examination (MMSE). Part of the test was to spell *world* backward, and always, with no hesitation, William would say "d-l-r-o-w!" Dr. Dreher would just shake his head.

May 5, 2005

Eating had become a struggle, so Ensure spiked with ice cream was welcomed. Instant breakfast with banana and several snacks a day helped. William didn't see things on his plate, so Arlyne handed these to him.

Taking medication had become a problem of sorts. William tried putting the pills in a glass of water to take, so Arlyne just waited to try again later. He lost twenty pounds but, at times, was still quite congenial.

May 10, 2005

William didn't understand Arlyne most of the time, although he would utter an uh-huh as if he did understand. His speech continued to get worse. It didn't seem that he knew Arlyne more times than when he did know her: "You are not my wife," and another day, she was Anna or Lana.

William could not find the bathroom by himself, and when he did, he walked past the commode. Perhaps he couldn't see it. The bladder incontinence was accelerating, and he also did not want to chew his food, bathe, and clean his teeth. William did not recognize his twenty-five-year-old granddaughter.

June 14, 2005

William began hallucinating in the evening. A lady was on top of the neighbor's small shed; then she was swinging. A turkey was on the rocker in the bedroom. He became hyperactive, flailing and overactive legs and arms, and ranted unintelligible utterances. He took four pills over sixteen hours, and then they were stopped. When he rose from the chair, he lost his balance and fell on the bedroom floor. It took two hours for Arlyne to get him up on the bed; he tried so hard to do what she asked but with little success.

It was now 3:00 a.m., and Arlyne thought it best to wait until 7:00 a.m. to call the doctor, who said to get him to the hospital. They were in the emergency room from 8:30 a.m. to 5:30 p.m., waiting for William to be admitted. William was in the hospital three days when a decision by doctors was made to send him to an assisted living facility because they felt he needed professional care.

Arlyne decided on the Gables for assisted living, which was only twenty minutes away. William was sedated and, therefore, was agreeable to all that was transpiring. Arlyne followed the ambulance in her car to the facility. (William had made a request for a "hankerfish" [handkerchief].) He had a private room and was ambulatory.

June 16, 2005

Aides said William did not eat well at breakfast or dinner, but for lunch, he ate everything in sight: soup with crackers in it, entrée, carton of milk, dessert plus Magic Cup supplement (312 calories). They gave him medicines: Tambocor, Synthroid, and hydroxyurea.

June 20, 2005

During the day, William didn't talk at all while Arlyne was there at 10:30 a.m. to 3:00 p.m. He ate very little. The daily routine ensued that Arlyne drove every day to the Gables at about 10:00 a.m., took care of him, and usually left around 3:00 p.m. Most people thought she was an employee there.

As time progressed, William's decline was becoming rather obvious. Arlyne would take him in a wheelchair for "walks" in the neighborhood or for a nap in the garden area. William also had rehab exercises, but that seemed to be an exercise in futility, and he didn't enjoy it at all. He wouldn't eat in the dining room either. William was ambulatory during the day and wandered all over, taking naps in other resident's beds, and didn't willingly participate in other activities.

Assisted living was, indeed, another journey of Alzheimer's behavior for William. Requiring cooperation and exposure to other persons' difficulties and activities added another dimension to his daily routine, both negative and positive.

Some of the other residents there were rather interesting.

In church at the Gables, Margaret was in the front row for the church services. Arlyne sat two rows behind her. Before services, Margaret decided she had on the wrong blouse and in no time had it pulled up to her neck. Arlyne broke the sound barrier in getting to her and helped her get the blouse back down.

Sybil was maybe sixty pounds, was in a wheelchair, and carried a stuffed animal around every day. When Arlyne arrived, Sybil said that her hair was so pretty.

And Arlyne replied, "You are a sweet, kind lady." Every day, every day.

At lunchtime, Sybil threw a glass of water on Raymond as he wheeled by, and she screamed, echoing off the walls, "If I get a hold of you, I'll kill you."

The next day, they had the same conversation with Arlyne about being sweet and kind, but Sybil hesitated and replied, "Not always."

Arlyne commented to herself, "I know what you mean!"

Betty was attractive, in a little girl way; she was four feet, five inches and must walk continuously all day, but sitting at lunch didn't seem to be a problem. Raymond was a slight, small, and mean-tempered man. And there was another man, Ward, who was just the opposite of Raymond—large and authoritative in style. Betty was standing up at the table, and Ward pushed her back down on the chair, hollering, "Sit down, Betty!"

At which time, he gave Raymond a terrific punch in the face, and a scuffle ensued. Next day, Raymond sported a mouse in the right eye.

Arlyne picked up William's jacket, which had a noticeable bulge in the pocket. Investigating, she found several socks rolled up; one had flowers on it, obviously not his, and in the other pocket were two pair of sunglasses, definitely not his. He never wore sunglasses.

Faye was maybe four feet and walked a lot, and they were unable to keep her from going in the kitchen area, taking food, and testing it by sticking her fingers in the food. She always had something to eat in her hand while walking. Trying to keep her out of the kitchen, the aides told her nicely to stay out, and she replied, "Bullshit."

Rusty was another little lady who walked all day and did hand modeling for Jergens lotion. She would see another person and put her hand out in greeting (the other hand hanging onto a railing). If she got your hand, she put a death grip on it. She never blinked. was that possible?

Stella shuffled wherever she went. Her joy was singing her favorite song "You Are My Sunshine" and getting some of the others to join her while waiting to be served lunch—over and over and over.

Al was a state trooper, was now in a wheelchair, and must be fed by his wife every day. Food had to be mashed, and then he got to choking, which became violent. As he coughed up the food, the sound revulsed most others in the area.

William was very well-behaved, comparatively speaking. It was rather depressing to go there for Arlyne, but she felt it was probably the best place for him for the care he needed. They put siderails on his bed so he didn't wander at night. However, he somehow wiggled and pushed his way out of the bars on the sides of the bed. Resourceful! There was a thermostat on the wall in his room, and he had dismantled it several times. Arlyne asked for it to remain dismantled.

November 25, 2005

On Thanksgiving Day, Arlyne was torn about deciding to take William home for the occasion or not. Perhaps he would have given her a hard time about returning to the facility. He had not left the facility to go home at all. Finally, Arlyne thought he would be pleased to go home and to go in the car, so she invited the family for dinner as well.

William had no idea where he was and didn't recognize even slightly, as they went in the driveway and approached the house. However, he had a seemingly happy and joyful time.

In the late afternoon, it approached the time to leave the house to return to the facility. Arlyne said happily that it was time for him to get in the car and go back to the Gables. No negativity showed in his behavior. William went without hesitation with Arlyne, who got him in the car, and they uneventfully arrived at the Gables. Arlyne got him out of the car there, walked him to his residence, got him undressed and dressed for bed, tucked him in, and said goodnight; and that was the end of a peaceful, wonderful day. It was also the last time for him to be at his home.

December 12, 2005

William was transported to Hunters Creek Rehab and Nursing Home.

December 23, 2005

The facility doctor was called, and they wanted to take William to the hospital. His white blood cell count was very high, his platelet count was very high, his urinalysis had a high potassium count, his kidney area was very sensitive, and he was catheterized for a urine sample. He might need more antibiotics. William had made his way out of bed and fell. Unbelievable how he accomplished this, but he did not further harm himself in any way.

December 24, 2005

Arlyne opted not to approve transport to the hospital and made an appointment with the hematologist. It was very difficult transporting William there and back; a neighbor friend helped with carrying William practically every step. Retrospectively, Arlyne felt, perhaps, it was a wrong decision. However, she imminently felt the pressing responsibility to seek added professional support. After a very serious conversation with the hematologist, he wrote down three dictates: "(1) Can continue chemo or not, (2) under no circumstances should William be hospitalized, (3) hospice and comfort care only."

How could this be happening? His days were few, and the future seemed an abyss. Despair and hopelessness could not give us comfort. Therefore, Arlyne must be strong to carry this burden.

"Be with me, Lord!" Arlyne loudly pleaded.

December 26, 2005

After William was transported to the nursing home, each day was a carbon copy of the previous days. Arlyne drove early each day to see him and performed the care and whatever it took to make William comfortable.

The aides continued to report that William refused to eat much, but ice cream was usually accepted.

A gigantic heartbreaking moment of Arlyne's daily arrival was delivered gently but was earth-shaking and undeniably audible: William smiled a welcoming upon her arrival, as though he really was happy to see her. "I don't know who you are. Who are you?"

Unable to control her emotions any longer, Arlyne quickly turned, left the room, and dissolved into body-trembling sobs and rivers of tears that just wouldn't stop.

"However can I accept this, Lord? It just can't be. Not after forty-four years of holding hands and meeting every earthly happening together. How can I possibly deal with this, God? Please, please help me," Arlyne pleaded over and over. The duty nurses circled the wagons with tea and sympathy, which was profoundly appreciated by Arlyne. Later, Arlyne reluctantly was able to gather her senses and return to William's room with a familiar demeanor, well aware of her immediate requirements and the futility ahead.

"Head up, shoulders back, chin in."

Let's get the wheelchair and go for a walk in the sun, Arlyne encouraged her inner self. Arlyne was often reminded and guided by the respective observations of Dr. Dreher and Peggy Bargmann: "Alzheimer's disease did not rob William of his essence."

"William never lost his identity. He never wavered from his beginnings."

May 20, 2006

It had been fifteen years since William was diagnosed, and the following days were recognizably downhill, but Arlyne was always praying for another good day. Since December 2005, when William first entered the nursing home, his weight went from 179 pounds to a haunting 135 pounds. One day, William didn't talk at all, while Arlyne carefully noticed that he ate some lunch but not the usual and seemed phlegmy and congested. William asked Arlyne to hold his hand. His eyes were not focusing, she also noticed.

Arlyne had come that morning at the usual 10:00 a.m., and at 3:00 p.m., when she was preparing to leave for the day, she stopped by the nurses' station and reported routinely but not aware of anything that had radically changed. Arlyne told the nurses that they might want to check his congestion.

At 8:00 p.m. that same day, Nurse Allison called Arlyne from the facility and reported that William was breathing very hard with oxygen level at 8 and a temperature of 103 degrees. She immediately left home and probably broke the speed limit getting to the facility. He was laboring to breathe, and although he had a DNR (do not resuscitate) in his records, Arlyne asked them, in order to ease the situation, to administer oxygen and a suppository to bring down his temperature. William's blood pressure was extremely high and then low. His breathing wasn't shaking his entire body. Then his breathing became very shallow, with some hesitation between breaths. William's nails turned blue, and it was soon 3:30 a.m. on May 21, 2006, that he took his last breath. Tightly holding his hands, Arlyne unwillingly accepted the finality of the moment. Her precious, wonderful husband was on his journey to the Lord's heavenly kingdom.

Please guide his journey, Lord.

Arlyne stayed with William until the funeral home arrived for his body. At this hour, 3:00 a.m. to 4:00 a.m., there was hardly anyone on duty to help her but a nurse and one aide. Not prepared for these extreme circumstances, Arlyne asked for some large maintenance plastic bags. She folded all his belongings, gathered up the remaining personal items, and piled them all in a wheelchair for transport to her car. Returning home about 4:30 a.m., her lonesome life had begun and was in high gear.

This had been the most dreaded moment of Arlyne's life—the passing of her beloved William into the Lord's heavenly kingdom. There was an inner feeling of relief, however, to know William was now released from the unrelenting, earthly shackles of the past fifteen years. Yet she wept, for she had to part with this very special person with whom she was blessed and who had been her love and her life.

5

Memoriam

In memoriam: Captain William R. O'Gara

A military memorial was held at Bushnell National Cemetery that included the family and USMMA representatives.

2012

Captain William R. O'Gara was honorarily inducted into the USMMA Hall of Outstanding Graduates, posthumously; and an exact copy of the bronze plaque was awarded to his wife, Arlyne.

May 15, 2012

Correspondence to Arlyne O'Gara
From: Ray La Hood, Secretary of Transportation, Washington, DC

Dear Mrs. O'Gara,

 Captain O'Gara's life is a wonderful illustration of the Academy's motto ACTA NON VERBA. As an alumnus, his distinguished accomplishments bring credit to King's Point and serve as an inspiration to the Regiment of Midshipmen.

Sincerely,
Ray La Hood

Arlyne and Captain William O'Gara, 2001

Memory Gardens, United States Merchant Marine Academy

Afterword

Not a burden but an opportunity

Understanding and evaluating our blessings are difficult requirements for assessments. Perhaps, at times, it is a beneficial, but arduous, journey to estimate and consider where our lives fit adequately in the worldly scheme. After all, and retrospectively, isn't the embodiment of life, on all levels, a comparison?

This has been a reverent unfolding of a worthwhile life of caring, loving, giving, curiosity, awareness, and profound faith; a contributory life of striving to use the best of God's given abilities, collectively exemplifying and promoting that internal flying bridge syndrome.

Acta non verba.

When anxiety was great within me, your consolation brought joy to my soul. (Psalm 94:19)

About the Author

Dr. Arlyne O'Gara told this flying bridge syndrome journey to A. D. Pforr. Arlyne was an educator, entrepreneur, community leader, and generous United States Merchant Marine Academy (USMMA) benefactor. She was married almost forty-five years to the late Captain William R. O'Gara '50 USMMA. Together, they achieved successes in cofounding two businesses. Arlyne self-owned Personnel Management Services, a human resources company; was a distinguished graduate of West Chester State University; had a master's degree from Villanova University, and had a doctoral degree from Temple University and Brunel University, London, England.

Her beloved husband succumbed to Alzheimer's disease at age seventy-eight after a life incredibly well lived. A passionate champion for persons with Alzheimer's, Arlyne established the O'Gara Library at the Alzheimer's Association, Central and North Florida Chapter, having six branches, and was a benefactor of Brain Fitness Academy. She also provided USMMA with a cultural and educational opportunity to learn more about Alzheimer's disease.

CPSIA information can be obtained
at www.ICGtesting.com
Printed in the USA
LVHW011039221121
704099LV00009B/202